PRESIDENCY IN THE UNITED STATES

PRESIDENTIAL APPOINTMENTS: OVERVIEW AND THE 110TH CONGRESS

PRESIDENCY IN THE UNITED STATES

Additional books in this series can be found on Nova's website under the Series tab.

Additional E-books in this series can be found on Nova's website under the E-books tab.

CONGRESSIONAL POLICIES, PRACTICES AND PROCEDURES

Additional books in this series can be found on Nova's website under the Series tab.

Additional E-books in this series can be found on Nova's website under the E-books tab.

PRESIDENCY IN THE UNITED STATES

PRESIDENTIAL APPOINTMENTS: OVERVIEW AND THE 110TH CONGRESS

CAROLINE P. DEMPSEY
AND
JONATHAN L. MILFORD
EDITORS

Nova Science Publishers, Inc.
New York

For permission to use material from this book please contact us:
Telephone 631-231-7269; Fax 631-231-8175
Web Site: http://www.novapublishers.com

NOTICE TO THE READER

Additional color graphics may be available in the e-book version of this book.

Library of Congress Cataloging-in-Publication Data

Presidential appointments : overview and the 110th Congress / editors,
Caroline P. Dempsey and Jonathan L. Milford.
p. cm.
Includes index.
ISBN 978-1-61324-067-0 (hardcover)
1. United States--Officials and employees--Selection and appointment. 2.
Legislative oversight--United States. I. Dempsey, Caroline P. II. Milford,
Jonathan L. III. Title.
JK731.P74 2011
352.6'50973--dc22
2011007140

Published by Nova Science Publishers, Inc. † New York

CONTENTS

PREFACE

The Constitution empowers the President to nominate and, by and with the advice and consent of the Senate, to appoint principal officers of the United States. This new book explains the process for filling positions to which the President makes appointments with the advice and consent of the Senate. It also identifies, for the 110th Congress, all nominations to executive-level full-time positions in the 15 departments.

Chapter 1- The appointment process for advice and consent positions consists of three main stages. The first stage is selection, clearance, and nomination by the President. This step includes preliminary vetting, background checks, and ethics checks of potential nominees. At this stage, the president may also consult with Senators who are from the same party if the position is located in a state. The second stage of the process is consideration of the nomination in the Senate, most of which takes place in committee. Finally, if a nomination is approved by the full Senate, the nominee is given a commission signed by the President, which makes the nomination official.

Chapter 2- The President makes appointments, with the advice and consent of the Senate, to some 152 full-time leadership positions on 34 federal regulatory and other collegial boards and commissions. This appointment process consists of three distinct stages: selection, clearance, and nomination by the President; consideration by the Senate; and appointment by the President. These advice and consent positions can also temporarily be filled by the President alone through a recess appointment. Membership positions on this set of collegial bodies often have fixed terms, and incumbents are often protected from arbitrary removal by the President. The enabling statutes for most of these boards and commissions require political party balance in their membership.

In: Presidential Appointments
Editors: C. P. Dempsey, J. L. Milford
ISBN: 978-1-61324-067-0

Chapter 1

PRESIDENTIAL APPOINTMENTS TO FULL-TIME POSITIONS IN EXECUTIVE DEPARTMENTS DURING THE 110TH CONGRESS, 2007-2008*

Henry B. Hogue, Maeve P. Carey and Maureen Bearden

SUMMARY

The appointment process for advice and consent positions consists of three main stages. The first stage is selection, clearance, and nomination by the President. This step includes preliminary vetting, background checks, and ethics checks of potential nominees. At this stage, the president may also consult with Senators who are from the same party if the position is located in a state. The second stage of the process is consideration of the nomination in the Senate, most of which takes place in committee. Finally, if a nomination is approved by the full Senate, the nominee is given a commission signed by the President, which makes the nomination official.

During the 110th Congress, the President submitted to the Senate 172 nominations to executive department full-time positions. Of these 172

* This is an edited, reformatted and augmented version of a Congressional Research Services publication, dated November 19, 2010.

nominations, 125 were confirmed; 13 were withdrawn; and 34 were returned to him in accordance with Senate rules. For those nominations that were confirmed, an average of 104 days elapsed between nomination and confirmation. The median number of days elapsed was 92.

The methodology used in this report to count the length of time between nomination and confirmation differs from that which was used in previous similar CRS reports. The statistics presented here include the days during which the Senate was adjourned for its summer recesses and between sessions of Congress. The methodological change, which may reduce the comparability of statistics in this report with those of the earlier research, is discussed in the text of this report as well as in an appendix. Reasons for the change include the conversion of long recesses into a series of short recesses punctuated by pro forma sessions during the 110th Congress; the fact that although committees may not be taking direct action on nominations in the form of hearings or votes, they are likely still considering and processing nominations during recesses; and a desire to be consistent with the methodology used by many political scientists as well as CRS research on judicial nominations. In addition, an argument could be made that the decision to extend Senate consideration of nominees over the course of a recess is intentional, and the choice to extend this length of time is better represented by including all days, including long recesses.

President George W. Bush did not make any recess appointments to executive department full-time positions during the 110th Congress.

Information for this report was compiled from data from the Senate nominations database of the Legislative Information System http://www.congress the *Congressional Record* (daily edition), the *Weekly Compilation of Presidential Documents*, telephone discussions with agency officials, agency websites, the *United States Code*, and the 2008 "Plum Book" (*United States Government Policy and Supporting Positions*).

INTRODUCTION

This report explains the process for filling positions to which the President makes appointments with the advice and consent of the Senate (PAS positions). It also identifies, for the 110th Congress, all nominations to executive-level full-time positions[1] in the 15 departments. Profiles of the departments provide information regarding their full-time PAS positions and related appointment activity during the 110th Congress.

The Appointment Process for Advice and Consent Positions

The President and the Senate share the power to appoint the principal officers of the United States.[2] The Constitution (Article II, Section 2, clause 2) empowers the President to nominate and, by and with the advice and consent of the Senate, to appoint the principal officers of the United States.[3] Three distinct stages mark the appointment process: selection, clearance, and nomination by the President; consideration by the Senate; and appointment by the President.

Selection, Clearance, and Nomination

In the first stage, the White House selects and clears a prospective appointee before sending a formal nomination to the Senate. There are a number of steps in this stage of the process for most Senate-confirmed positions. First, with the assistance of, and preliminary vetting by, the White House Office of Presidential Personnel, the President selects a candidate for the position. Members of Congress and interest groups sometimes recommend candidates for specific PAS positions. They may offer their suggestions by letter, for example, or by contact with a White House liaison.[4] In general, the White House is under no obligation to follow such recommendations. In the case of the Senate, however, it has been argued that Senators are constitutionally entitled, by virtue of the advice and consent clause noted above, to provide advice to the President regarding his selection; the extent of this entitlement is a matter of some debate.[5] As a practical matter, in instances where Senators perceive insufficient pre-nomination consultation has occurred, they have sometimes exercised their procedural prerogatives to delay or even effectively block consideration of a nomination.[6]

During the clearance process, the candidate prepares and submits several forms, including the "Public Financial Disclosure Report" (Standard Form (SF) 278), the "Questionnaire for National Security Positions" (SF 86), and the White House "Personal Data Statement Questionnaire." The Office of the Counsel to the President oversees the clearance process, which often includes the collection and review of background information by the Federal Bureau of Investigation (FBI), Internal Revenue Service (IRS), Office of Government Ethics (OGE), and an ethics official for the agency to which the candidate is to be appointed. If conflicts of interest are found during the background check, OGE and the agency ethics officer may work with the candidate to mitigate the conflicts. Once the Office of the Counsel to the President has cleared the candidate, the nomination is ready to be submitted to the Senate.

The selection and clearance stage has often been the longest part of the appointment process. There have been, at times, lengthy delays, particularly when many candidates have been processed simultaneously, such as at the beginning of an Administration, or where conflicts needed to be resolved. Candidates for higher-level positions have often been accorded priority in this process. At the end of 2004, in an effort to reduce the elapsed time between a new President's inauguration and the appointment of his or her national security team, Congress enacted amendments to the Presidential Transition Act of 1963.[7] These amendments encourage a President-elect to submit, for security clearance, potential nominees to high-level national security positions as soon as possible after the election.[8] A separate provision of law, enacted as part of the Federal Vacancies Reform Act of 1998, lengthens, during presidential transitions, the potential duration of a temporary appointment by 90 days.[9] Although this provision might give some additional flexibility to an incoming President, it might also lengthen the appointment process for some positions by, in effect, extending the deadline by which a permanent appointment must be completed.

For a position located within a state (e.g., U.S. attorney, U.S. marshal, and U.S. district judge), the President, by custom, normally has nominated an individual recommended by one or both Senators (if they are from the same party as the President) from that state. In instances where neither Senator is from the President's party, he usually has deferred to the recommendations of party leaders from the state. Occasionally, the President has solicited recommendations from Senators of the opposition party because of their positions in the Senate.

If circumstances permit and conditions are met, the President could give the nominee a recess appointment to the position (see section entitled "Recess Appointments" below). Recess appointments have sometimes had political consequences, however, particularly where Senators perceived that such an appointment was an effort to circumvent their constitutional role. Some Senate-confirmed positions, such as many of those in the executive departments, may also be temporarily filled under the Vacancies Act.[10]

A nominee has no legal authority to assume the duties and responsibilities of the position; a nominee who is hired by the agency as a consultant while awaiting confirmation may serve only in an advisory capacity. Authority to act comes once there is Senate confirmation and presidential appointment, or if another method of appointment, such as a recess appointment or a temporary appointment, is utilized. (For further information on these methods, see sections entitled "Recess Appointments" and "Temporary Appointments" below.)

Senate Consideration

In the second stage, the Senate alone determines whether or not to confirm a nomination.[11] The way the Senate has acted on a nomination has depended largely on the importance of the position involved, existing political circumstances, and policy implications. Generally, the Senate has shown particular interest in the nominee's views and how they are likely to affect public policy.[12] Two other factors have sometimes affected the examination of a nominee's personal and professional qualities: whether the President's party controlled the Senate, and the degree to which the President became involved in supporting the nomination.

Much of the Senate confirmation process occurs at the committee level. Administratively, nominations are received by the Senate executive clerk, who arranges for the referral of the nominations to committee, according to the Senate rules and precedents.[13] Committee nomination activity has generally included investigation, hearing, and reporting stages. As part of investigatory work, committees have drawn on information provided by the White House, as well as information they themselves have collected. Some committees have held hearings on nearly all nominations; others have held hearings for only some. Hearings provide a public forum to discuss a nomination and any issues related to the program or agency for which the nominee would be responsible. Even where confirmation has been thought to be a virtual certainty, hearings have provided Senators and the nominee with opportunities to go on the record with particular views or commitments. Senators have used hearings to explore nominees' qualifications, articulate policy perspectives, or raise related oversight issues.

A committee may decline to act on a nomination at any point—upon referral, after investigation, or after a hearing. If the committee votes to report a nomination to the full Senate, it has three options: it may report the nomination favorably, unfavorably, or without recommendation. A failure to obtain a majority on the motion to report means the nomination will not be reported to the Senate.[14] If the committee declines to report a nomination, the

Senate may, under certain circumstances, discharge the committee from further consideration of the nomination in order to bring it to the floor.[15]

The Senate historically has confirmed most, but not all, executive nominations. Rarely, however, has a vote to confirm a nomination failed on the Senate floor. Unsuccessful nominations usually do not make it past the committee stage. Failure of a nomination to make it out of committee has occurred for a variety of reasons, including opposition to the nomination, inadequate amount of time for consideration of the nomination, or factors that may not be directly related to the merits of the nomination.

Senate rules provide that "[n]ominations neither confirmed nor rejected during the session at which they are made shall not be acted upon at any succeeding session without being again made to the Senate by the President."[16] In practice, such pending nominations have been returned to the President at the end of the session or Congress. Pending nominations also may be returned automatically to the President at the beginning of a recess of more than 30 days, but the Senate rule providing for this return is often waived.[17]

Appointment

In the final stage, the confirmed nominee is given a commission bearing the Great Seal of the United States signed by the President and is sworn into office. The President may sign the commission at any time after confirmation, at which point the appointment becomes official. Once the appointee is given the commission and sworn in, he or she has full authority to carry out the responsibilities of the office.

Recess Appointments

The Constitution also empowers the President to make limited-term appointments without Senate confirmation when the Senate is in recess.[18] Such recess appointments expire at the end of the next session of the Senate. Appendix C provides a table showing the dates of the Senate recesses for the 110th Congress and showing that during this Congress, President Bush made no recess appointments to executive department positions.

Presidents have occasionally used the recess appointment power to circumvent the confirmation process. In response, Congress has enacted provisions that restrict the pay of recess appointees under certain circumstances. Because most potential appointees to full-time positions cannot serve without a salary, the President has an incentive to use his recess appointment authority in ways that allow them to be paid. Under the provisions, if the position falls vacant while the Senate is in session and the President fills it by recess appointment, the appointee may not be paid from the Treasury until he or she is confirmed by the Senate. However, the salary prohibition does not apply

1) if the vacancy arose within 30 days before the end of the session of the Senate;
2) if, at the end of the session, a nomination for the office, other than the nomination of an individual appointed during the preceding recess of the Senate, was pending before the Senate for its advice and consent; or
3) if a nomination for the office was rejected by the Senate within 30 days before the end of the session and an individual other than the one whose nomination was rejected thereafter receives a recess appointment.[19]

A recess appointment falling under any one of these three exceptions must be followed by a nomination to the position not later than 40 days after the beginning of the next session of the Senate.[20] For this reason, when a recess appointment is made, the President generally submits a new nomination for the nominee even when an old nomination is pending.[21] These provisions have been interpreted by the Department of Justice to preclude payment of an appointee who is given successive recess appointments to the same position.[22]

Although recess appointees whose nominations to a full term are subsequently rejected by the Senate may continue to serve until the end of their recess appointment, a provision of the FY2008 Financial Services and General Government Appropriations Act may prevent them from being paid after their rejection. The provision reads, "Hereafter, no part of any appropriation contained in this or any other Act shall be paid to any person for the filling of any position for which he or she has been nominated after the Senate has voted not to approve the nomination of said person."[23] Prior to this provision, similar wording was included in annual funding measures for most or all of the previous 50 years.

Another recent congressional response to the President's use of recess appointments was the decision, during the latter part of the first session of the 110th Congress, to restructure the Senate's longer recesses into a series of shorter recesses divided by pro forma sessions.[24] Based upon the notion that the President can be restricted from making recess appointments during a recess that is no more than three days, the Senate sought to prevent recess appointments by holding pro forma sessions approximately every three days.[25] Beginning in November of 2007, the Senate agreed to regularly scheduled pro forma sessions during periods that would have otherwise been recesses of duration of a week or longer. The Senate recessed on November 16, and pro forma meetings were convened on November 20, 23, 27, and 29, with no business conducted. The Senate reconvened and conducted business beginning on December 3, 2007. Similar procedures were followed for the remainder of the 110th Congress during other periods that would otherwise have been Senate recesses of at least a week in duration. For the remainder of his presidency, President Bush did not make any more recess appointments.[26]

Temporary Appointments

Congress has provided limited statutory authority for the temporary filling of vacant positions requiring Senate confirmation. It is expected that, in general, officials holding PAS positions who have been designated as "acting" are holding their offices under this authority or other statutory authority specific to their agencies. Under the Federal Vacancies Reform Act of 1998,[27] when an executive agency position requiring confirmation becomes vacant, it may be filled temporarily in one of three ways: (1) the first assistant to such a position may automatically assume the functions and duties of the office; (2) the President may direct an officer in any agency who is occupying a position requiring Senate confirmation to perform those tasks; or (3) the President may select any officer or employee of the subject agency who is occupying a position for which the rate of pay is equal to or greater than the minimum rate of pay at the GS-15 level, and who has been with the agency for at least 90 of the preceding 365 days. The temporary appointment is for 210 days, but the time restriction is suspended if a first or second nomination for the position is pending. In addition, during a presidential transition, the 210-day restriction period does not begin to run until either 90 days after the President assumes office, or 90 days after the vacancy occurs, if it is within the 90-day inauguration period. The act does not apply to positions on multiheaded regulatory boards and commissions and to certain other specific positions that may be filled temporarily under other statutory provisions.[28]

APPOINTMENTS DURING THE 110TH CONGRESS

Table 1 summarizes appointment activity, during the 110th Congress, related to full-time positions in the 15 departments. President George W. Bush submitted to the Senate 172 nominations to executive department full-time positions. Of these 172 nominations, 125 were confirmed; 13 were withdrawn; and 34 were returned to the President under the provisions of Senate rules.[29]

President Bush did not make any recess appointments to the departments during this period.

LENGTH OF TIME TO CONFIRM A NOMINATION

The length of time a given nomination may be pending in the Senate has varied widely. Some nominations were confirmed within a few days, others were confirmed within several months, and some were never confirmed. This report provides, for each executive department nomination that was confirmed in the 110th Congress, the number of days between nomination and confirmation ("days to confirm"). For confirmed nominations, an average (mean) of 104 days elapsed between nomination and confirmation. The median number of days elapsed was 92.

The methodology used in this report to count the length of time between nomination and confirmation differs from that which was used in previous similar CRS reports. The statistics presented here include the days during which the Senate was adjourned for its summer recesses and between sessions of Congress. The methodological change reduces the direct comparability of statistics in this report with those of the earlier research. Reasons for the change include the conversion of long recesses into a series of short recesses punctuated by pro forma sessions during the 110th Congress; the fact that although committees may not be taking direct action on nominations in the form of hearings or votes, they are likely still considering and processing nominations during recesses; and a desire to be consistent with the methodology used by a majority of political scientists as well as CRS research on judicial nominations. In addition, an argument could be made that the decision to extend Senate consideration of nominees over the course of a recess is intentional, and the choice to extend this length of time is better represented by including all days, including long recesses. A more detailed explanation of this methodological change is located in **Appendix E**.

Table 1. Nomination Action for 15 Departments During the 110th Congress.

Positions in the 15 departments (total)	364
Positions to which nominations were made	156[a]
Individual nominees	167[b]
Nominations submitted to the Senate during the 110th Congress (total)	172[b]
Disposition of nominations	
Confirmed by the Senate	125
Withdrawn	13
Returned (total)	34
End of the 1st session of the 110th Congress	2
End of the 2nd session of the 110th Congress	32
Recess Appointments (total)	0

Source: Table developed by the Congressional Research Service using data presented in the appendices of this report.

a One of the positions, the Department of Veterans' Affairs' Assistant Secretary for Congressional Affairs, was filled twice during the 110th Congress. Thomas E. Harvey was confirmed for the position on May 25, 2007, and then Christine O. Hill was confirmed on October 2, 2008 after Harvey left the position. This is counted as a single position in the total count of positions to which nominations were made. Considering this a separate position, since there was a second successful nomination, would bring this count of positions to which nominations were made up to 157.

b The figures shown here reveal that there is a distinction between the number of positions to which nominations were made (156), the number of individual nominees (167), and the total number of nominations submitted (172). The number of positions to which nominations were made (156) differs from the number of individual nominees (167) for two reasons. First, the President sometimes nominated more than one individual successively to an open position, usually following the return or withdrawal of his original nomination. Second, less frequently, the President nominated a single individual to more than one position over the course of the Congress. Again, this usually followed the return or withdrawal of the first nomination. The number of total nominations submitted (172) is higher than both of these numbers because it includes cases in which the President nominated an individual to the same position more than once. For example, Anita K. Blair was nominated for positions three times during the 110th Congress. Two of these nominations were to the same position in the Navy (but both nominations were unsuccessful and returned to the President), and the third was to a position in the Air Force. This would count as two positions to which nominations were made, one individual nominee, and three nominations submitted total.

Organization of This Chapter

Executive Department Profiles

Each of the 15 executive department profiles provided in this report is organized into two parts: a table providing information, as of the end of the 110th Congress, regarding the organization's full-time PAS positions, and a table listing nominations and appointments to these positions during the 110th Congress. Data for these tables were collected from several authoritative sources.[30]

The first of these two tables identifies, as of the end of the 110th Congress,[31] each full-time PAS position in the department,[32] its incumbent, and its pay level. For most presidentially appointed positions requiring Senate confirmation, the pay levels fall under the Executive Schedule, which, as of January 2009, ranged from level I ($196,700) for Cabinet-level offices to level V ($143,500) for the lowest-ranked positions. An incumbent's name followed by "(A)" indicates an official who was, at that time, serving in an acting capacity. Vacancies are also noted in the first table.

The appointment action table provides, in chronological order, information concerning each nomination. It shows the name of the nominee, position involved, date of nomination or appointment, date of confirmation, and number of days between receipt of a nomination and confirmation. Actions other than confirmation (i.e., nominations returned to or withdrawn by the President) are also noted. Some individuals were nominated more than once for the same position, usually because the first nomination was returned to the President.

Each appointment action table provides the average "days to confirm" in two ways: mean and median. Both are presented because the mean can be influenced by outliers in the data, while the median does not tend to be influenced by outliers. In other words, a nomination that took an extraordinarily long time might cause a significant change in the mean, but the median would be unaffected. Presenting both numbers is a better way to look at the central tendency of the data.

For a small number of positions in this report, the two tables may give slightly different titles to the same position. This is a result of the fact that the titles used in the nomination the White House submits to the Senate, the title of each position as established by statute, and the title of the position used by the department itself are not always identical. The first table presented for each department, the table listing the incumbents at the end of the 110th Congress, relies upon data provided by the department itself in listing the positions. The second table presented, the list of nomination action within each department, relies primarily upon the Senate nominations database of the Legislative Information System (LIS).[33] This information is based upon the nomination sent to the Senate by the White House, which is not always identical to the exact title of the position used by the department. However, the inconsistency only appears in a small minority of the positions listed in this report. Inconsistencies are noted in the footnotes following each appointment table.

Additional Appointment Information

Appendix A presents a table of all nominations and recess appointments to positions in executive departments, alphabetically organized by last name, and follows a similar format to that of the department appointment action tables. It identifies the agency involved and the dates of nomination and confirmation. The table also indicates if a nomination was confirmed, withdrawn, or returned. The mean and median numbers of days taken to confirm a nomination are also provided.

Appendix B provides a table with summary information on appointments and nominations, by department. For each of the 15 executive departments discussed in this report, the table provides the number of positions, nominations, individual nominees, confirmations, nominations returned, and nominations withdrawn. The table also provides the mean and median numbers of days to confirm a nomination.

Appendix C provides a table showing the dates of the Senate recesses for the 110th Congress.

A list of department abbreviations can be found in Appendix D.

As noted above, this report employs certain methods that differ from reports tracking appointments during previous Congresses. These methodological changes are explained in detail in Appendix E.

Department of Agriculture (USDA)

Full-Time PAS Positions, as of the End of the 110th Congress.

Position	Incumbent	Pay Level
Secretary	Ed Schafer	I
Deputy Secretary	Charles F. Conner	II
Inspector Generala	Phyllis K. Fong	a
Under Secretary – Farm and Foreign Agricultural Services	Mark E. Keenum	III
Under Secretary – Food, Nutrition, and Consumer Services	Nancy Montanez-Johner	III
Under Secretary – Food Safety	Elizabeth Johnson (A)b	III
Under Secretary – Marketing and Regulatory Programs	Bruce I. Knight	III
Under Secretary – Natural Resources and Environment	Mark E. Rey	III
Under Secretary – Research, Education, and Economics	Gale A. Buchanan	III
Under Secretary – Rural Development	Douglas L. Faulkner (A)[b]	III
Assistant Secretary – Administration	Boyd K. Rutherford	IV
Assistant Secretary – Civil Rights	Margo M. McKay	IV
Assistant Secretary – Congressional Relations	Linda A. Strachan	IV
Chief Financial Officer[c]	Charles R. Christopherson Jr.	IV
General Counsel	Marc L. Kesselman	IV
Administrator – Rural Utilities Services	James M. Andrew	IV

a The President may remove an inspector general (IG) from office, as he may remove most other appointed officials in the departments. In the case of an IG, however, the law provides that "[i]f an Inspector General is removed from office or is transferred to another position or location within an establishment, the President shall communicate in writing the reasons for any such removal or transfer to both Houses of Congress, not later than 30 days before the removal or transfer." (5 U.S.C. Appx. § 3 (b)). Under the provisions of 5 U.S.C. Appx. § 3 (e), "The annual rate of basic pay for an inspector general (as defined under section 12(3)) shall be the rate payable for level III of the Executive Schedule under section 5314 of title 5, United States Code, plus 3 percent."

b Johnson was named as acting in a September 25, 2008 USDA press release. Faulkner was named as acting in a December 23, 2008, USDA press release.

c The chief financial officer (CFO) may be appointed by the President, with the advice and consent of the Senate, or may be designated by the President from among agency officials who have been confirmed by the Senate for other positions (31 U.S.C. § 901(a)(1)).

USDA Nomination Action During the 110th Congress.

Nominee	Position	Nominated	Confirmed	Days to Confirm
Ed Schafer	Secretary	12/06/07	01/28/08	53

DEPARTMENT OF COMMERCE (DOC)

Full-Time PAS Positions, as of the End of the 110th Congress.

Position[a]	Incumbent	Pay Level
Secretary	Carlos M. Gutierrez	I
Deputy Secretary	John J. Sullivan	II
Under Secretary – Economic Affairs	Cynthia A. Glassman	III
Under Secretary – Export Administration[b]	Mario Mancuso	III
Under Secretary – Intellectual Property/Director - U.S. Patent and Trademark Office	Jonathan W. Dudas	III
Under Secretary – International Trade	Christopher A. Padilla	III
Under Secretary – Oceans and	William J. Brennan (A)	III
Atmosphere/Administrator – National Oceanic and Atmospheric Administration (NOAA)		
Inspector General[c]	Todd J. Zinser	[c]
Assistant Secretary – Administration/Chief Financial Officer[d]	Otto J. Wolff	IV
Assistant Secretary – Communications and Information	Meredith A. Baker (A)	IV
Assistant Secretary – Economic Development	Santanu K. Baruah	IV
Assistant Secretary – Export Administration	Matthew S. Norman (A)	IV
Assistant Secretary – Export Enforcement	Darryl W. Jackson	IV
Assistant Secretary – Import Administration	David M. Spooner	IV
Assistant Secretary – Legislative and Intergovernmental Affairs	Nathaniel F. Wienecke	IV
Assistant Secretary – Manufacturing and Services	William G. Sutton Jr.	IV
Assistant Secretary – Market Access and Compliance	David S. Bohigian	IV
Assistant Secretary – Oceans and Atmosphere/Deputy Administrator – NOAA	William J. Brennan	IV
Assistant Secretary – Trade Promotion/Director General – U.S. and Foreign Commercial Service	Israel Hernandez	IV
Director – U.S. Census Bureau	Steven H. Murdock	IV
Director – National Institute of Standards and Technology	Vacant	IV
General Counsel	Lily F. Claffee	IV
Chief Scientist – NOAA[e]	Vacant	V

a Positions in this column do not include those in the commissioned officer corps of the National Oceanic and Atmospheric Administration (NOAA).

b Within the Department of Commerce, this position is also sometimes known as Under Secretary of Industry and Security.

c The President may remove an inspector general (IG) from office, as he may remove most other appointed officials in the departments. In the case of an IG, however, the law provides that "[i]f an Inspector General is removed from office or is transferred to another position or location within an establishment, the President shall communicate in writing the reasons for any such removal or transfer to both Houses of Congress, not later than 30 days before the removal or transfer." (5 U.S.C. Appx. § 3 (b)). Under the provisions of 5 U.S.C. Appx. § 3 (e), "The annual rate of basic pay for an inspector general (as defined under section 12(3)) shall be the rate payable for level III of the Executive Schedule under section 5314 of title 5, United States Code, plus 3 percent."

d The chief financial officer (CFO) may be appointed by the President, with the advice and consent of the Senate, or may be designated by the President from among agency officials who have been confirmed by the Senate for other positions (31 U.S.C. § 901(a)(1)). Wolff was separately nominated and confirmed to be CFO and to be Assistant Secretary for Administration in the 107th Congress.

e According to an agency spokesperson, this position had not been filled since 1996.

DOC Nomination Action During the 110th Congress.

Nominee	Position	Nominated	Confirmed	Days to
Jane C. Luxton	Asst. Secy. – Oceans and	01/09/07	Withdrawn 05/03/07	
Mario Mancuso	Under Secy. – Export	01/18/07	05/25/07	127
William G. Sutton	Asst. Secy. –	05/07/07	08/03/07	88
Steven H.	Dir. – Censusb	06/18/07	12/19/07	184
Christopher A.	Under Secy. – International	09/04/07	12/19/07	106
Todd J. Zinser	Inspector General	09/07/07	12/19/07	103
John J. Sullivan	Deputy Secretary	12/04/07	03/13/08	100
William J.	Asst. Secy. – Oceans and	01/22/08	06/04/08	134
Neil S. Patel	Asst. Secy. –	03/05/08	Returned 01/02/09[c]	
Lily F. Claffee	General Counsel	03/31/08	06/04/08	65
Christopher R.	Asst. Secy. – Export	03/31/08	06/27/08	88
Mean number of days to confirm a nomination				111
Median number of days to confirm a nomination				103

a Within the Department of Commerce, this position is also sometimes known as Under Secretary for Industry and Security.

b As noted in the text of this report, position titles occasionally differ across the two tables provided for each department. In the Commerce Department, the Director of the U.S. Census Bureau (listed in the incumbents table above) is the same position as the Director of the Census listed in this nomination table.

c Returned to the President at the end of the 110th Congress under the provisions of Senate Rule XXXI, paragraph 6 of the Standing Rules of the Senate.

Department of Defense (DOD)

Full-Time PAS Positions, as of the End of the 110th Congress.

Position	Incumbent	Pay Level
Secretary	Robert M. Gates	I
Deputy Secretary	Gordon England	II
Under Secretary – Acquisition, Technology, and Logistics	John J. Young Jr.	II
Under Secretary – Comptroller/Chief Financial Officer[a]	Tina W. Jonas	III
Under Secretary – Intelligence	James R. Clapper Jr.	III
Under Secretary – Personnel and Readiness	David S. C. Chu	III
Under Secretary – Policy	Eric S. Edelman	III
Deputy Under Secretary – Acquisition and Technology	James I. Finley	III
Deputy Under Secretary – Logistics and Materiel Readiness	P. Jackson Bell	III
Inspector General[b]	Gordon S. Heddell (A)	b
Principal Deputy Under Secretary – Personnel and Readiness	Michael L. Domiguez	IV
Principal Deputy Under Secretary – Policy	Christopher R. Henry	IV
Assistant Secretary – Asian and Pacific Security Affairs[c]	James Shinn	IV
Assistant Secretary – Health Affairs	S. Ward Casscells	IV
Assistant Secretary – Homeland Defense	Paul McHale	IV
Assistant Secretary – International Security Affairs	Mary Beth Long	IV
Assistant Secretary – International Security Policy	Joseph A. Benkert	IV
Assistant Secretary – Legislative Affairs	Robert L. Wilkie	IV
Assistant Secretary – Networks and Information Integration	John G. Grimes	IV
Assistant Secretary – Public Affairs	Robert Hastings	IV
Assistant Secretary – Reserve Affairs	Thomas F. Hall	IV
Assistant Secretary – Special Operations and Low- Intensity Conflict	Michael G. Vickers	IV
Director – Defense Research and Engineering	Vacant	IV

Position	Incumbent	Pay Level
Director – Operational Test and Evaluationd	Charles E. McQueary	IV
General Counsel	Daniel J. Dell'Orto (A)	IV
Assistant to the Secretary – Nuclear and Chemical and Biological Defense Programs	Frederick S. Celec	V
Department of the Air Force Secretary		
	Michael B. Donley	II
Under Secretary	Vacant	IV
Assistant Secretary – Acquisition	Sue C. Payton	IV
Assistant Secretary – Financial Management/Comptroller	John H. Gibson	IV
Assistant Secretary – Manpower and Reserve Affairs	Craig W. Duehring	IV
Assistant Secretary – Installations, Environment, and Logistics	Kevin W. Billings	IV
General Counsel	Mary L. Walker	IV
Department of the Army		
Secretary	Preston M. Geren	II
Under Secretary	Nelson M. Ford	IV
Assistant Secretary – Civil Works	John P. Woodley Jr.	IV
Assistant Secretary – Financial Management/Comptroller	Peter Kunkel (A)	IV
Assistant Secretary – Installations and Environment	Keith E. Eastin	IV
Assistant Secretary – Manpower and Reserve Affairs	Ronald J. James	IV
Assistant Secretary – Acquisition, Logistics, and Technology	Dean G. Popps (A)	IV
General Counsel	Benedict S. Cohen	IV
Department of the Navy		
Secretary	Donald C. Winter	II
Under Secretary	Dionel M. Aviles	IV
Assistant Secretary – Financial Management/Comptroller	Douglas A. Brook	IV
Assistant Secretary – Installations and Environment	Buddie J. Penn	IV
Assistant Secretary – Manpower and Reserve Affairs	Anita K. Blair (A)	IV
Assistant Secretary – Research, Development, and Acquisition	Sean J. Stackley	IV

Full-Time PAS Positions, as of the End of the 110th Congress (Continued).

Position	Incumbent	Pay Level
General Counsel	Frank R. Jimenez	IV
Joint Chiefs of Staffe Chairman Vice Chairman Chief of Staff (Air Force) Chief of Staff (Army) Chief of Naval Operations Commandant of the Marine Corps	Michael G. Mullen James E. Cartwright Norton A. Schwartz George W. Casey Jr. Gary Roughead James T. Conway	(Members of the Joint Chiefs of Staff are compensated under the military pay system, rather than the executive schedule.)

a The chief financial officer (CFO) may be appointed by the President, with the advice and consent of the Senate, or may be designated by the President from among agency officials who have been confirmed by the Senate for other positions (31 U.S.C. § 901(a)(1)). In the 108th Congress, Jonas was confirmed to be Under Secretary of Defense/Comptroller, and she also served as CFO.

b The President may remove an inspector general (IG) from office, as he may remove most other appointed officials in the departments. In the case of an IG, however, the law provides that "[i]f an Inspector General is removed from office or is transferred to another position or location within an establishment, the President shall communicate in writing the reasons for any such removal or transfer to both Houses of Congress, not later than 30 days before the removal or transfer." (5 U.S.C. Appx. § 3 (b)). Under the provisions of 5 U.S.C. Appx. § 3 (e), "The annual rate of basic pay for an inspector general (as defined under section 12(3)) shall be the rate payable for level III of the Executive Schedule under section 5314 of title 5, United States Code, plus 3 percent."

c The position of Assistant Secretary of Asian and Pacific Security Affairs in the Department of Defense was filled for the first time during the 110th Congress. The position was established by the John Warner National Defense Authorization Act during the 109th Congress on Oct. 17, 2006 (P.L. 109-364, Div A, Title IX, Subtitle A, § 901(a); 120 Stat. 2350).

d The President may remove the Director of Operational Test and Evaluation from office. The law provides that "The President shall communicate the reasons for any such removal to both Houses of Congress." (10 U.S.C. § 139(a)(1).

e The chairman and vice chairman serve two-year terms; other members serve four-year terms.

DOD Nomination Action During the 110th Congress.

Nominee	Positions	Nominated	Confirmed	Days to
Anita K. Blair	Asst. Secy. – Air Force –	01/09/07	Withdrawn 09/18/07	
Michael J. Burns	Asst. to the Secretary – Nuclear	01/09/07	Withdrawn 06/11/07	
James R. Clapper Jr.	Under Secy. – Intelligence	01/29/07	04/11/07	72
S. Ward Casscells	Asst. Secy. – Health Affairs	02/26/07	03/29/07	31
Claude M. Kicklighter	Inspector General	02/26/07	04/12/07	45
Michael G. Vickers	Asst. Secy. – Special Operations	04/10/07	07/23/07	104
Preston M. Geren	Secretary – Army	05/24/07	07/13/07	50
Douglas A. Brook	Asst. Secy. – Navy – Financial	06/05/07	11/16/07	164
John J. Young Jr.	Under Secy. – Acquisition,	06/21/07	11/16/07	148
Anita K. Blair	Asst. Secy. – Navy – Manpower	09/18/07	Returned 12/31/07[a]	
James Shinn	Asst. Secy. – Asian and Pacific	10/23/07	12/19/07	57
John H. Gibson	Asst. Secy. – Air Force –	10/26/07	12/19/07	54
Mary Beth Long	Asst. Secy. – International	11/08/07	12/19/07	41
Craig W. Duehring	Asst. Secy. – Air Force –	11/15/07	12/19/07	34
Nelson M. Ford	Under Secy. – Army	01/22/08	07/23/08	183
Anita K. Blair	Asst. Secy. – Navy – Manpower	01/23/08	Returned 01/02/09[b]	
Joseph A. Benkert	Asst. Secy. – International	02/25/08	07/23/08	149
Sean J. Stackley	Asst. Secy. – Navy – Research,	05/01/08	07/23/08	83
Frederick S. Celec	Asst. to the Secretary – Nuclear	06/10/08	07/23/08	43
Michael B. Donley	Secretary – Air Force	06/25/08	10/02/08	99
Robert Hastings	Asst. Secy. – Public Affairs	07/10/08	Returned 01/02/09[b]	
Mean number of days to confirm a nomination			85	
Median number of days to confirm a nomination			65	

a Returned to the President at the end of the first session of the 110th Congress under the provisions of Senate rule XXXI, paragraph 6 of the Standing Rules of the Senate.

b Returned to the President at the end of the 110th Congress under the provisions of the Senate Rule XXXI, paragraph 6 of the Standing Rules of the Senate.

DEPARTMENT OF EDUCATION (ED)

Full-Time PAS Positions, as of the End of the 110th Congress.

Position	Incumbent	Pay Level
Secretary	Margaret Spellings	I
Deputy Secretary	Raymond J. Simon	II
Director – Institute of Education Sciences[a]	Sue Betka (A)	II
Under Secretary	Kent D. Talbert (A)	III
Inspector General[b]	Jerry G. Bridges (A)	b
Chief Financial Officer[c]	Thomas Skelly (A)	IV
Assistant Secretary – Civil Rights	Stephanie J. Monroe	IV
Assistant Secretary – Communications and Outreach	Meredith Beaton (A)	IV
Assistant Secretary – Elementary and Secondary	Kerri L. Briggs	IV
Assistant Secretary – Legislation and Congressional Affairs	Holly A. Kuzmich	IV
Assistant Secretary – Management	Christopher M. Marston	IV
Assistant Secretary – Planning, Evaluation and Policy Development	Williamson Evers	IV
Assistant Secretary – Postsecondary Education	Cheryl Oldham (A)	IV
Assistant Secretary – Special Education and Rehabilitative Services	Tracy R. Justesen	IV
Assistant Secretary – Vocational and Adult Education	Troy R. Justesen	IV
General Counsel	Kent D. Talbert	IV
Commissioner – Education Statistics[d]	Stuart Kerachsky (A)	IV
Commissioner – Rehabilitation Services Administration	Edward Anthony (A)	V

a This position has a six-year term and specified qualifications. See 20 U.S.C. § 9514(b, d).

b The President may remove an inspector general (IG) from office, as he may remove most other appointed officials in the departments. In the case of an IG, however, the law provides that "[i]f an Inspector General is removed from office or is transferred to another position or location within an establishment, the President shall communicate in writing the reasons for any such removal or transfer to both Houses of Congress, not later than 30 days before the removal or transfer." (5 U.S.C. Appx. § 3 (b)). Under the provisions of 5 U.S.C. Appx. § 3 (e), "The annual rate of basic pay for an inspector general (as defined under section 12(3)) shall be the rate payable for level III of the Executive Schedule under section 5314 of title 5, United States Code, plus 3 percent."

c The chief financial officer (CFO) may be appointed by the President, with the advice and consent of the Senate, or may be designated by the President from among agency officials who have been confirmed by the Senate for other positions (31 U.S.C. § 901(a)(1)). In previous Congresses, the

CFO for the Department of Education has been appointed by the President, with the advice and consent of the Senate.

d This position has a six-year term and specified qualifications. See 20 U.S.C. §9517(b).

ED Nomination Action During the 110th Congress.

Nominee	Position	Nominated	Confirmed	Days to
Williamson	Asst. Secy. – Planning,	02/08/07	10/16/07	250
Kerri L. Briggs	Asst. Secy. – Elementary and	03/07/07	06/22/07	107
Diane A. Jones	Asst. Secy. – Postsecondary	05/22/07	08/01/07	71
Tracy R.	Asst. Secy. – Special Education	11/15/07	12/19/07	34
Holly A.	Asst. Secy. – Legislation and	06/24/08	08/01/08	38
Christopher M.	Asst. Secy. – Management	06/24/08	08/01/08	38
Jerry G. Bridges	Inspector General	09/09/08	Returned 01/02/09[a]	
Mean number of days to confirm a nomination			90	
Median number of days to confirm a nomination			55	

a. Returned to the President at the end of the 110th Congress under the provisions of Senate Rule XXXI, paragraph 6 of the Standing Rules of the Senate.

DEPARTMENT OF ENERGY (DOE)

Full-Time PAS Positions, as of the End of the 110th Congress.

Position	Incumbent	Pay Level
Secretary	Samuel W. Bodman	I
Deputy Secretary	Jeffrey F. Kupfer (A)	II
Under Secretary	Clarence H. Albright Jr.	III
Under Secretary – Nuclear Security/Administrator – National Nuclear Security Administration (NNSA)	Thomas P. D'Agostino	III
Under Secretary – Science	Raymond L. Orbach	III
Inspector General[a]	Gregory H. Friedman	a
Principal Deputy Administrator – NNSA	William C. Ostendorff	IV
Deputy Administrator – Defense Programs, NNSA	Robert L. Smolen	IV
Deputy Administrator – Defense Nuclear Nonproliferation, NNSA	William H. Tobey	IV
Administrator – Energy Information Administration	Howard Gruenspecht (A)	IV
Assistant Secretary – Congressional and Intergovernmental Affairs	Lisa E. Epifani	IV

Full-Time PAS Positions, as of the End of the 110th Congress (Continued).

Position	Incumbent	Pay Level
Assistant Secretary – Electricity Delivery and Energy Reliability	Kevin M. Kolevar	IV
Assistant Secretary – Energy Efficiency and Renewable Energy	John F. Mizroch (A)	IV
Assistant Secretary – Environmental Management	Ines Triay (A)	IV
Assistant Secretary – Fossil Energy	James A. Slutz (A)	IV
Assistant Secretary – Nuclear Energy	Dennis R. Spurgeon	IV
Assistant Secretary – Policy and International Affairs	Jonathan Shrier (A)	IV
Chief Financial Officer[b]	Steven J. Isakowitz	IV
Director – Office of Civilian Radioactive Waste Management	Edward F. Sproat III	IV
Director – Office of Minority Economic Impact and Diversity	Theresa Alvillar-Speake	IV
Director – Office of Science	Raymond L. Orbach	IV
General Counsel	David R. Hill	IV

a. The President may remove an inspector general (IG) from office, as he may remove most other appointed officials in the departments. In the case of an IG, however, the law provides that "[i]f an Inspector General is removed from office or is transferred to another position or location within an establishment, the President shall communicate in writing the reasons for any such removal or transfer to both Houses of Congress, not later than 30 days before the removal or transfer." (5 U.S.C. Appx. § 3 (b)). Under the provisions of 5 U.S.C. Appx. § 3 (e), "The annual rate of basic pay for an inspector general (as defined under section 12(3)) shall be the rate payable for level III of the Executive Schedule under section 5314 of title 5, United States Code, plus 3 percent."

b. The chief financial officer (CFO) may be appointed by the President, with the advice and consent of the Senate, or may be designated by the President from among agency officials who have been confirmed by the Senate for other positions (31 U.S.C. § 901(a)(1)).

DOE Nomination Action During 110th Congress.

Nominee	Position	Nominated	Confirmed	Days to Confirm
Kevin M. Kolevar	Asst. Secy. – Electricity Delivery and Energy Reliability	01/09/07	08/03/07	206
Steven J. Isakowitz	Chief Financial Officer	02/08/07	05/25/07	106
William C. Ostendorff	Principal Deputy Administrator, NNSA	02/26/07	03/29/07	31
Thomas P. D'Agostino	Under Secy. – Nuclear Security/Admin., NNSA[a]	05/21/07	08/01/07	72
Lisa E. Epifani	Asst. Secy. – Congressional and Intergovernmental Affairs	06/13/07	08/03/07	51
Clarence H. Albright Jr.	Under Secy.	06/21/07	08/03/07	43
Robert L. Smolen	Deputy Admin. – Defense Programs, NNSA	07/31/07	11/16/07	108
Stanley C. Suboleski	Asst. Secy. – Fossil Energy	12/11/07	Withdrawn 02/26/08	
J. Gregory Copeland	General Counsel	01/22/08	Withdrawn 06/24/08	
Jeffrey F. Kupfer	Deputy Secy.	04/02/08	Returned 01/02/09[b]	
James A. Slutz	Asst. Secy. – Fossil Energy	07/30/08	Returned 01/02/09[b]	
F. Chase Hutto III	Asst. Secy. – International Affairs and Domestic Policy	09/26/08	Returned 01/02/09[b]	
Mean number of days to confirm a nomination			88	
Median number of days to confirm a nomination			72	

a NNSA: National Nuclear Security Administration

b Returned to the President at the end of the 110th Congress under the provisions of Senate Rule XXXI, paragraph 6 of the Standing Rules of the Senate.

DEPARTMENT OF HEALTH AND HUMAN SERVICES (HHS)

Full-Time PAS Positions, as of the End of the 110th Congress.

Position[a]	Incumbent	Pay Level
Secretary	Michael O. Leavitt	I
Deputy Secretary	Tevi D. Troy	II
Administrator – Centers for Medicare and Medicaid Services	Kerry Weems (A)	III
Inspector General[b]	Daniel R. Levinson	b
Administrator – Substance Abuse and Mental Health Services Administration	Eric Broderick (A)	IV
Assistant Secretary – Aging	Josefina G. Carbonell	IV
Assistant Secretary – Children and Families	Daniel C. Schneider (A)	IV
Assistant Secretary – Health	Joxel Garcia	c
Assistant Secretary – Legislation	Vincent J. Ventimiglia Jr.	IV
Assistant Secretary – Planning and Evaluation	Benjamin E. Sasse	IV
Assistant Secretary – Preparedness and Response[d]	W. Craig Vanderwagen	IV
Assistant Secretary – Public Affairs	Christina H. Pearson	IV
Assistant Secretary – Resources and Technology/Chief Financial Officer[e]	Charles E. Johnson	IV
Commissioner – Food and Drug Administration	Andrew C. von Eschenbach	IV
Director – National Institutes of Health	Raynard S. Kington (A)	IV
General Counsel	Preeya M. Noronha (A)	IV
Commissioner – Children, Youth, and Families	Joan E. Ohl	V
Commissioner – Administration for Native Americans	Quanah C. Stamps	V
Director – Indian Health Service[f]	Robert G. McSwain	V
Surgeon General[g]	Steven K. Galson (A)	h

a The positions in this column do not include officers of the U.S. Public Health Service Commissioned Corps, except in cases where such a commission is incidental to the position listed.

b The President may remove an inspector general (IG) from office, as he may remove most other appointed officials in the departments. In the case of an IG, however, the law provides that "[i]f an Inspector General is removed from office or is transferred to another position or location within an establishment, the President shall communicate in writing the reasons for any such removal or transfer to both Houses of Congress, not later than 30 days before the removal or transfer." (5 U.S.C. Appx. § 3 (b)). Under the provisions of 5 U.S.C. Appx. § 3 (e), "The annual rate of basic pay for an inspector general (as defined under section 12(3)) shall be the rate payable for level III of the Executive Schedule under section 5314 of title 5, United States Code, plus 3 percent."

c The Assistant Secretary for Health was compensated as a commissioned officer at Level 0-10 (37 U.S.C. § 201).

d The position of Assistant Secretary for Preparedness and Readiness was established by P.L. 109-417, Title 1, § 102(a)(3); (120 Stat. 2833). The position was first filled in the 110th Congress as shown.

e The chief financial officer (CFO) may be appointed by the President, with the advice and consent of the Senate, or may be designated by the President from among agency officials who have been confirmed by the Senate for other positions (31 U.S.C. § 901(a)(1)). Department representatives have indicated that the positions were combined as noted in the table.

f This position has a four-year term; a Director may serve more than one term. See 25 U.S.C. § 1661(a).

g This position has a four-year term and specified qualifications. See 42 U.S.C. § 205.

h The Surgeon General is compensated as a commissioned officer at Level 0-9 (37 U.S.C. § 201).

HHS Nomination Action During the 110th Congress.

Nominee	Position	Nominated	Confirmed	Days to Confirm
Daniel Meron	General Counsel	01/09/07	Returned 01/02/09[a]	
W. Craig Vanderwagen	Asst. Secy. – Preparedness and Response	02/12/07	03/21/07	37
Tevi D. Troy	Deputy Secy.	05/03/07	08/03/07	92
Charles W. Grim	Director – Indian Health Service	05/21/07	Withdrawn 09/04/07	
James W. Holsinger Jr.	Surgeon General	05/24/07	Returned 01/02/09a	
Diane D. Rath	Asst. Secy. – Family Supportb	07/11/07	Returned 01/02/09a	
Benjamin E. Sasse	Asst. Secy. – Planning and Evaluation	07/26/07	12/19/07	146
Christina H. Pearson	Asst. Secy. – Public Affairs	09/25/07	12/19/07	85
Robert G. McSwain	Director – Indian Health Service	12/19/07	04/29/08	132
Joxel Garcia	Asst. Secy. – Health	01/22/08	03/13/08	51
Mean number of days to confirm a nomination				91
Median number of days to confirm a nomination				89

a Returned to the President at the end of the 110th Congress under the provisions of Senate Rule XXXI, paragraph 6 of the Standing Rules of the Senate.

b As noted in the text of this report, position titles occasionally differ across the two tables provided for each department. In the Health and Human Services Department, the Assistant Secretary for Children and Families (listed in the incumbents table above) is the same position as the Assistant Secretary for Family Support listed in this nomination table.

DEPARTMENT OF HOMELAND SECURITY (DHS)

Full-Time PAS Positions, as of the End of the 110th Congress.

Position[a]	Incumbent	Pay Level
Secretary	Michael Chertoff	I
Deputy Secretary	Paul A. Schneider	II
Under Secretary – Management	Elaine C. Duke	III
Under Secretary – National Protection and Programs	Robert D. Jamison	III
Under Secretary – Science and Technology	Jay M. Cohen	III
Director – U.S. Citizenship and Immigration Services	Michael Aytes (A)	III
Commissioner – U.S. Customs and Border Protection	W. Ralph Basham	III
Inspector General[b]	Richard L. Skinner	b
Assistant Secretary – Policy	Stewart A. Baker	IV
Assistant Secretary – U.S. Immigration and Customs	John P. Torres (A)	IV
Assistant Secretary – Transportation Security	Edmund S. "Kip" Hawley	IV
Administration		
Assistant Secretary – Health Affairs and Chief Medical	Jeffrey W. Runge	IV
Officerc		
Chief Financial	Peggy Sherry (A)	IV
General Counsel	Gus P. Coldebella (A)	IV
Commandant of the Coast Guard	Thad W. Allen	Admiral[c]
Director - Office of Counternarcotics Enforcement	Uttam Dhillon	IV
Federal Emergency Management Agency		
Administrator[f]	R. David Paulison	II
Deputy Administrator – National Preparedness[c]	Dennis Schrader	III
Deputy Administrator/Chief Operating Officer[c]	Harvey E. Johnson Jr.	III
Assistant Administrator – Grants Program Directorate[c]	W. Ross Ashley III	IV
United States Fire Administrator	Gregory B. Cade	IV

a. The Post-Katrina Emergency Management Reform Act of 2006 (Title VI of P.L. 109-295), enacted October 4, 2006, included provisions that established, abolished, and changed certain advice and consent positions at DHS. The act established, as PAS positions, an administrator of the Federal Emergency Management Agency (FEMA) (6 U.S.C. § 313(c)); four FEMA deputy administrators (6 U.S.C. § 321c(a)); and a chief medical officer for the department (6 U.S.C. § 321e(a)). It abolished the position of Under Secretary for Federal Emergency Management (6 U.S.C. § 113(a)). During the departmental reorganization that followed the act, the DHS Office of Grants and Training, which had been headed by an assistant secretary, was transferred to FEMA, within DHS, as the Office of Grants Programs. The head of this renamed office was retitled as the Assistant Administrator for Grant Programs. (See U.S. Department of Homeland Security, letter from Secretary Michael Chertoff to the Honorable Joseph I. Lieberman, Chairman, Committee on Homeland Security and Governmental Affairs, U.S. Senate, Washington, DC, January 18, 2007 (identical letter sent to other congressional leaders). Of the four FEMA deputy administrators, only the positions in use at the end of the 110th Congress are shown. Additionally, the Homeland Security Act (P.L. 107-296, § 103; 116 Stat. 2135) provided for "Not more than 12 Assistant Secretaries" appointed through the advice and consent process. Of these, only the positions in use at the end of the 110th Congress are shown. Some assistant secretary positions previously created under this authority, such as the Assistant Secretary for Border and Transportation Security Policy, no longer exist, as such.

b The President may remove an inspector general (IG) from office, as he may remove most other appointed officials in the departments. In the case of an IG, however, the law provides that "[i]f an Inspector General is removed from office or is transferred to another position or location within an establishment, the President shall communicate in writing the reasons for any such removal or transfer to both Houses of Congress, not later than 30 days before the removal or transfer." (5 U.S.C. Appx. § 3 (b)). Under the provisions of 5 U.S.C. Appx. § 3 (e), "The annual rate of basic pay for an inspector general (as defined under section 12(3)) shall be the rate payable for level III of the Executive Schedule under section 5314 of title 5, United States Code, plus 3 percent."

c This position, filled for the first time in the 110th Congress, is discussed in footnote a, above.

d The chief financial officer (CFO) may be appointed by the President, with the advice and consent of the Senate, or may be designated by the President from among agency officials who have been confirmed by the Senate for other positions (31 U.S.C. § 901(a)(1)).

e The Commandant of the Coast Guard is compensated as a commissioned officer with the rank of Admiral at Level 0-10 (37 U.S.C. § 201).

f During the departmental reorganization that followed the Post-Katrina Act, it was determined that R. David Paulison, who had been confirmed as Under Secretary for Federal Emergency Management, would continue to lead FEMA in the new position of Administrator. (See page 3 of the letter from Secretary Michael Chertoff to specified members of Congress cited in footnote a, above.)

DHS Nomination Action During 110th Congress.

Nominee	Position	Nominated	Confirmed	Days to Confirm
Gregory B. Cade	Admin. – U.S. Fire Administration[a]	01/09/07	05/25/07	136
Julie L. Myers	Asst. Secy. – U.S. Immigration and Customs Enforcement	01/09/07	12/19/07	344
Jeffrey W. Runge	Asst. Secy. – Health Affairs and Chief Medical Officer	08/02/07	12/19/07	139
Robert D. Jamison	Under Secy. – National Protection and Programs	09/04/07	Withdrawn 12/19/07	
Harvey E. Johnson Jr.	Deputy Admin./ Chief Operating Officer – Federal Emergency Management Agency	09/07/07	Withdrawn 12/12/07	
Gus P. Coldebella	General Counsel	10/16/07	Returned 01/02/09b	
Harvey E. Johnson Jr.[c]	Deputy Admin. – Federal Emergency Management Agency	12/12/07	06/27/08	198
Robert D. Jamison	Under Secy. – National Protection and Programs	12/19/07	12/19/07	0
Paul A. Schneider	Deputy Secy.	02/26/08	06/04/08	99
Elaine C. Duke	Under Secy. – Management	04/02/08	06/27/08	86
Jonathan R. Scharfen	Dir. – U.S. Citizenship and Immigration Services	10/01/08	Returned 01/02/09[b]	
Mean number of days to confirm a nomination			143	
Median number of days to confirm a nomination			136	

a As noted in the text of this report, position titles occasionally differ across the two tables provided for each department. In the Homeland Security Department, the United States Fire Administrator (listed in the incumbents table above) is the same position as the Administrator for the U.S. Fire Administration listed in this nomination table.

b Returned to the President at the end of the 110th Congress under the provisions of Senate Rule XXXI, paragraph 6 of the Standing Rules of the Senate.

c Harvey E. Johnson Jr. was originally nominated to serve as FEMA's Deputy Administrator and its Chief Operating Officer. After the White House withdrew the nomination and submitted a second nomination for Johnson to only the Deputy Administrator position, he was successfully confirmed.

DEPARTMENT OF HOUSING AND URBAN DEVELOPMENT (HUD)

Full-Time PAS Positions, as of the End of the 110th Congress.

Position	Incumbent	Pay Level
Secretary	Steven C. Preston	I
Deputy Secretary	Romolo "Roy" A. Bernardi	II
Director – Office of Federal Housing Enterprise Oversight[a]	James B. Lockhart III	II
Inspector General[b]	Kenneth M. Donohue Sr.	b
Assistant Secretary – Administration	Keith A. Nelson	IV
Assistant Secretary – Community Planning and Development	Susan D. Peppler	IV
Assistant Secretary – Congressional and Intergovernmental Relations	Sheila M. Greenwood	IV
Assistant Secretary – Fair Housing and Equal Opportunity	Kim Kendrick	IV
Assistant Secretary – Housing/Federal Housing Commissioner	Brian D. Montgomery	IV
Assistant Secretary – Policy Development and Research	Darlene F. Williams	IV
Assistant Secretary – Public Affairs	Vacant	IV
Assistant Secretary – Public and Indian Housing	Vacant	IV
Chief Financial Officer[c]	John W. Cox	IV
General Counsel	Michael C. Flynn (A)	IV
President – Government National Mortgage Association	Joseph J. Murin	IV

a This position has a five-year term and specified qualifications. See 12 U.S.C. § 4512.

b The President may remove an inspector general (IG) from office, as he may remove most other appointed officials in the departments. In the case of an IG, however, the law provides that "[i]f an Inspector General is removed from office or is transferred to another position or location within an establishment, the President shall communicate in writing the reasons for any such removal or transfer to both Houses of Congress, not later than 30 days before the removal or transfer." (5 U.S.C. Appx. § 3 (b)). Under the provisions of 5 U.S.C. Appx. § 3 (e), "The annual rate of basic pay for an inspector general (as defined under section 12(3)) shall be the rate payable for level III of the Executive Schedule under section 5314 of title 5, United States Code, plus 3 percent."

c The chief financial officer (CFO) may be appointed by the President , with the advice and consent of the Senate, or may be designated by the President from among agency officials who have been confirmed by the Senate for other positions (31 U.S.C. § 901(a)(1)). Cox was confirmed as HUD's CFO in the 109th Congress.

HUD Nomination Action During the 110th Congress.

Nominee	Position	Nominated	Confirmed	Days to Confirm
Scott A. Keller	Asst. Secy. – Congressional and Intergovernmental Affairs	01/09/07	Withdrawn 09/04/07	
Robert M. Couch	General Counsel	04/10/07	06/13/07	64
Joseph J. Murin	President – Government National Mortgage Association	10/16/07	06/27/08	255
Susan D. Peppler	Asst. Secy. – Community Planning and Development	02/06/08	06/27/08	142
Sheila M. Greenwoo d	Asst. Secy. – Congressional and Intergovernmental Relations	02/26/08	06/27/08	122
Steven C. Preston	Secretary	05/01/08	06/04/08	34
Mean number of days to confirm a nomination				123
Median number of days to confirm a nomination				122

DEPARTMENT OF THE INTERIOR (DOI)

Full-Time PAS Positions, as of the End of the 110th Congress.

Position	Incumbent	Pay Level
Secretary	Dirk Kempthorne	I
Deputy Secretary	P. Lynn Scarlett	II

Full-Time PAS Positions, as of the End of the 110th Congress (Continued).

Position	Incumbent	Pay Level
Special Trustee for American Indians	Ross O. Swimmer	a
Inspector Generalb	Earl E. Devaney	b
Assistant Secretary – Fish, Wildlife, and Parks	R. Lyle Laverty	IV
Assistant Secretary – Indian Affairs	George T. Skibine (A)	IV
Assistant Secretary – Land and Minerals Management	C. Stephen Allred	IV
Assistant Secretary – Policy, Management, and Budget/Chief Financial Officer[c]	Vacant[d]	IV
Assistant Secretary – Water and Science	Kameran L. Onley (A)	IV
Chairman – National Indian Gaming Commissione	Philip N. Hogen	IV
Solicitor	David L. Bernhardt	IV
Director – National Park Service	Mary A. Bomar	V
Director – Office of Surface Mining Reclamation and Enforcement	Brent T. Wahlquist (A)	V
Commissioner – Bureau of Reclamation	Robert W. Johnson	V
Director – Bureau of Land Management	James L. Caswell	V
Director – U.S. Fish and Wildlife Service	H. Dale Hall	V
Director – U.S. Geological Survey	Mark Myers	V
Commissioner -Indian Affairs[f]	Vacant	V

a The Special Trustee is to be paid "at a rate determined by the Secretary to be appropriate for the position, but not less than the rate of basic pay payable at Level II of the Executive Schedule..." (25 U.S.C. § 4042).

b The President may remove an inspector general (IG) from office, as he may remove most other appointed officials in the departments. In the case of an IG, however, the law provides that "[i]f an Inspector General is removed from office or is transferred to another position or location within an establishment, the President shall communicate in writing the reasons for any such removal or transfer to both Houses of Congress, not later than 30 days before the removal or transfer." (5 U.S.C. Appx. § 3 (b)). Under the provisions of 5 U.S.C. Appx. § 3 (e), "The annual rate of basic pay for an inspector general (as defined under section 12(3)) shall be the rate payable for level III of the Executive Schedule under section 5314 of title 5, United States Code, plus 3 percent."

c The chief financial officer (CFO) may be appointed by the President, with the advice and consent of the Senate, or may be designated by the President from among agency officials who have been confirmed by the Senate for other positions (31 U.S.C. § 901(a)(1)).

d The previous individual who held the position of Assistant Secretary for Policy, Management and Budget also served as the Chief Financial Officer. Because this Assistant Secretary position was vacant after that individual left the department, so was the position of the Chief Financial Officer.

e This position has a three-year term, specified qualifications. The President's removal power is limited. See 25 U.S.C. § 2704(b).

f This position (provided for at 25 U.S.C. § 1) had been vacant since 1981.

DOI Nomination Action During the 110th Congress.

Nominee	Position	Nominated	Confirmed	Days to Confirm
Carl Joseph Artman	Asst. Secy. – Indian Affairs	01/09/07	03/05/07	55
John Ray Correll	Dir. – Office of Surface Mining Reclamation and Enforcement	01/09/07	Withdrawn 06/28/07	
R. Lyle Laverty	Asst. Secy. – Fish and Wildlifea	03/26/07	10/29/07	217
James L. Caswell	Dir. – Bureau of Land Management	06/04/07	08/03/07	60
Brent T. Wahlquist	Dir. – Office of Surface Mining Reclamation and Enforcement	06/28/07	08/03/07	36
Kameran L. Onley	Asst. Secy. – Water and Science	03/31/08	Returned 01/02/09b	
Mean number of days to confirm a nomination		92		
Median number of days to confirm a nomination		58		

a As noted in the text of this report, position titles occasionally differ across the two tables provided for each department. In the Interior Department, the Assistant Secretary for Fish, Wildlife, and Parks (listed in the incumbents table above) is the same position as the Assistant Secretary for Fish and Wildlife listed in this nomination table.

b Returned to the President at the end of the 110th Congress under the provisions of Senate Rule XXXI, paragraph 6 of the Standing Rules of the Senate.

DEPARTMENT OF JUSTICE (DOJ)

Full-Time PAS Positions, as of the End of the 110th Congress.

Position[a]	Incumbent	Pay Level
Attorney General	Michael B. Mukasey	I
Deputy Attorney General	Mark R. Filip	II
Director – Federal Bureau of Investigation[b]	Robert S. Mueller III	II
Administrator – Drug Enforcement	Michele M. Leonhart (A)	III
Associate Attorney General	Kevin J. O'Connor	III
Solicitor General	Gregory G. Garre	III
Director – Bureau of Alcohol, Tobacco, Firearms, and Explosives[c]	Michael J. Sullivan (A)	III
Inspector General[d]	Glenn A. Fine	d
Assistant Attorney General – Antitrust Division	Deborah A. Garza (A)	IV
Assistant Attorney General – Civil Division	Gregory G. Katsas	IV
Assistant Attorney General – Civil Rights Division	Grace C. Becker (A)	IV
Assistant Attorney General – Criminal Division	Matthew W. Friedrich (A)	IV
Assistant Attorney General – Environment and Natural Resources Division	Ronald J. Tenpas	IV
Assistant Attorney General – Legislative Affairs	Keith B. Nelson (A)	IV
Assistant Attorney General – National Security Division	J. Patrick Rowan	IV
Assistant Attorney General – Office of Justice Programs	Jeffrey L. Sedgwick	IV
Assistant Attorney General – Office of Legal Counsel	Steven G. Bradbury (A)	IV
Assistant Attorney General – Office of Legal Policy	Elisebeth C. Cook	IV
Assistant Attorney General – Tax Division	Nathan J. Hochman	IV
Administrator – Office of Juvenile Justice and Delinquency Prevention	J. Robert Flores	IV
Deputy Administrator – Drug Enforcement Administration	Michele M. Leonhart	IV
Director – Bureau of Justice Assistance	Domingo S. Herraiz	IV
Director – Bureau of Justice Statistics	Michael Sinclair (A)	IV
Director – Community Relations Service[e]	Ondray T. Harris	IV
Director – National Institute of Justice	David W. Hagy	IV

Full-Time PAS Positions, as of the End of the 110th Congress (Continued).

Position	Incumbent	Pay Level
Director – Office for Victims of Crime	John W. Gillis	IV
Director – U.S. Marshals Service	John F. Clark	IV
Special Counsel – Immigration-Related Unfair Employment Practices[f]	Patrick P. Shen	g
Director -Violence Against Women Office	Cynthia Dyer	V

a Does not include U.S. attorney and U.S. marshal positions. The position of chief financial officer (CFO) is also not listed here. Although the Department of Justice is included in the statute that provides presidentially appointed and Senate-confirmed CFOs for all of the major executive branch agencies (31 U.S.C. § 901(a)(1)), this provision is superseded by 28 U.S.C. § 507. The latter section provides that the Assistant Attorney General for Administration, appointed by the Attorney General with the approval of the President, shall be the CFO for the Department of Justice.

b This position has a 10-year term. See 28 U.S.C. § 532 note.

c The position of Director – Bureau of Alcohol, Tobacco, Firearms, and Explosives became a presidential appointment with Senate confirmation position (PAS) in P.L. 109-177, Title V § 504 (120 Stat. 247). As of the end of the 110th Congress, the position had not been filled through the advice and consent process.

dThe President may remove an inspector general (IG) from office, as he may remove most other appointed officials in the departments. In the case of an IG, however, the law provides that "[i]f an Inspector General is removed from office or is transferred to another position or location within an establishment, the President shall communicate in writing the reasons for any such removal or transfer to both Houses of Congress, not later than 30 days before the removal or transfer." (5 U.S.C. Appx. § 3 (b)). Under the provisions of 5 U.S.C. Appx. § 3 (e), "The annual rate of basic pay for an inspector general (as defined under section 12(3)) shall be the rate payable for level III of the Executive Schedule under section 5314 of title 5, United States Code, plus 3 percent."

e This position has a four-year term. See 42 U.S.C. § 2000g.

f This position has a four-year term. See 8 U.S.C. § 1324b(c)(1).

g "The Special Counsel for Immigration-Related Unfair Employment Practices is entitled to receive compensation at a rate not to exceed the rate now or hereafter provided for grade GS-17 of the General Schedule," under 8 U.S.C. § 1324b(c)(3). In 1990, Sec. 529 of P.L. 101-509 converted the GS-16, GS-17, and GS-18 positions to Senior Level (SL) positions for the purposes of pay (5 U.S.C. § 5376). With regard to pay for such positions, the Plum Book states, "Pay for SL [Senior Level] positions ranges from 120 percent of the rate of basic pay for GS-15, step 1 to the rate payable for level IV of the Executive Schedule. ... SL employees are entitled to locality-based comparability payments for their respective locality pay area. The employee's locality rate of pay may not exceed the pay for level III of the Executive Schedule" (p. 203).

DOJ Nomination Action During the 110th Congress.

Nominee	Position	Nominated	Confirmed	Days to Confirm
William W. Mercer	Associate Attorney General	01/09/07	Withdrawn 06/25/07	
Steven G. Bradbury	Asst. Atty. General – Office of Legal Counsel	01/09/07	Returned 12/31/07[a]	
Patrick P. Shen	Special Counsel for Immigration-Related Unfair Employment Practices	01/18/07	10/04/07	259
Michael J. Sullivan	Dir. – Bureau of Alcohol, Tobacco, Firearms, and Explosives	03/22/07	Returned 01/02/09[b]	
Ondray T. Harris	Dir. – Community Relations Service	05/23/07	03/13/08	295
Ronald J. Tenpas	Asst. Atty. General – Environment and Natural Resources Division	06/04/07	12/13/07	192
David W. Hagy	Dir. – National Institute of Justice	06/05/07	03/13/08	282
Cynthia Dyer	Dir. – Violence Against Women Office	08/20/07	12/19/07	121
Michael B. Mukasey	Attorney General	09/21/07	11/08/07	48
Nathan J. Hochman	Asst. Atty. General – Tax Division	11/15/07	12/19/07	34
Grace C. Becker	Asst. Atty. General – Civil Rights Division	11/15/07	Returned 01/02/09[b]	
Mark R. Filip	Deputy Attorney General	12/05/07	03/03/08	89
Gregory G. Katsas	Asst. Atty. General – Civil Division	12/11/07	06/27/081	99
Kevin J. O'Connor	Associate Attorney General	12/11/07	04/01/08	112
Steven G. Bradbury	Asst. Atty. General – Office of Legal Counsel	01/23/08	Returned 01/02/09[b]	
Elisebeth C. Cook	Asst. Atty. General – Office of Legal Policy	01/30/08	06/04/08	126
Michele M. Leonhart	Admin. – Drug Enforcement	04/15/08	Returned 01/02/09[b]	
Jeffrey L. Sedgwick	Asst. Atty. General – Office of Justice Programs	04/23/08	10/02/08	162
J. Patrick Rowan	Asst. Atty. General – National Security Division	06/19/08	09/26/08	99
Gregory G. Garre	Solicitor General	06/19/08	10/02/08	105

DOJ Nomination Action During the 110th Congress (Continued).

Nominee	Position	Nominated	Confirmed	Days to Confirm
Matthew W. Friedrich	Asst. Atty. General – Criminal Division	12/11/08	Returned 01/02/09[b]	
Mean number of days to confirm a nomination			152	
Median number of days to confirm a nomination			124	

a Returned to the President at the end of the first session of the 110th Congress under the provisions of Senate Rule XXXI, paragraph 6 of the Standing Rules of the Senate.

b Returned to the President at the end of the 110th Congress under the provisions of Senate Rule XXXI, paragraph 6 of the Standing Rules of the Senate.

DEPARTMENT OF LABOR (DOL)

Full-Time PAS Positions, as of the End of the 110th Congress.

Position	Incumbent	Pay Level
Secretary	Elaine L. Chao	I
Deputy Secretary	Howard M. Radzely	II
Inspector General[a]	Gordon S. Heddell	[a]
Assistant Secretary – Administration and Management	Patrick Pizzella	IV
Assistant Secretary – Congressional and Intergovernmental Affairs	Kristine A. Iverson	IV
Assistant Secretary – Disability Employment Policy	Neil Romano	IV
Assistant Secretary – Employee Benefits Security Administration	Bradford P. Campbell	IV
Assistant Secretary – Employment and Training Administration	Brent R. Orrell (A)	IV
Assistant Secretary – Employment Standards Administration	Victoria A. Lipnic	IV
Assistant Secretary – Mine Safety and Health	Richard E. Stickler (A)	IV
Assistant Secretary – Occupational Safety and Health Administration	Thomas M. Stohler (A)	IV
Assistant Secretary – Public Affairs	David W. James	IV
Assistant Secretary – Policy	Leon R. Sequeira	IV
Assistant Secretary – Veterans' Employment and Training Service	Charles S. Ciccolella	IV

Full-Time PAS Positions, as of the End of the 110th Congress (Continued).

Position	Incumbent	Pay Level
Chief Financial Officer[b]	Douglas W. Webster	IV
Commissioner – Bureau of Labor Statistics[c]	Keith D. Hall	IV
Solicitor	Gregory F. Jacob	IV
Administrator – Wage and Hour Division	Alexander Passantino (A)	V
Director – Women's Bureau[d]	Shinae Chun	[e]

a The President may remove an inspector general (IG) from office, as he may remove most other appointed officials in the departments. In the case of an IG, however, the law provides that "[i]f an Inspector General is removed from office or is transferred to another position or location within an establishment, the President shall communicate in writing the reasons for any such removal or transfer to both Houses of Congress, not later than 30 days before the removal or transfer." (5 U.S.C. Appx. § 3 (b)). Under the provisions of 5 U.S.C. Appx. § 3 (e), "The annual rate of basic pay for an inspector general (as defined under section 12(3)) shall be the rate payable for level III of the Executive Schedule under section 5314 of title 5, United States Code, plus 3 percent."

b The chief financial officer (CFO) may be appointed by the President, with the advice and consent of the Senate, or may be designated by the President from among agency officials who have been confirmed by the Senate for other positions (31 U.S.C. § 901(a)(1)). Webster was confirmed as CFO in the 110th Congress.

c This position has a four-year term. See 29 U.S.C. § 3.

d By statute, the incumbent must be a woman (29 U.S.C. § 12).

e According to the 2008 Plum Book, the Director of the Women's Bureau was a Senior Level (SL) position (p. 108). With regard to pay for such positions, the Plum Book states, "Pay for SL [Senior Level] positions ranges from 120 percent of the rate of basic pay for GS-15, step 1 to the rate payable for level IV of the Executive Schedule. ... SL employees are entitled to locality-based comparability payments for their respective locality pay area. The employee's locality rate of pay may not exceed the pay for level III of the Executive Schedule" (p. 203). See also 5 U.S.C. 5376 and 5 U.S.C. 5304(g)(2).

DOL Nomination Action During the 110th Congress.

Nominee	Position	Nominated	Confirmed	Days to Confirm
Paul DeCamp	Administrator – Wage and Hour Division	01/09/07	Withdrawn 02/07/08	
Leon R. Sequeira	Asst. Secy. – Policy	01/09/07	02/15/07	37
Richard Stickler	Asst. Secy. – Mine Safety and Health	01/09/07	Returned 01/02/09[a]	
Bradford P. Campbell	Asst. Secy. – Employee Benefits Security Administration	05/03/07	08/03/07	92
Howard Radzely	Deputy Secretary	05/10/07	12/19/07	223
David W. James	Asst. Secy. – Public Affairs	06/18/07	08/03/07	46
Gregory F. Jacob	Solicitor	09/04/07	12/19/07	106
Keith Hall	Commissioner – Labor Statistics	09/18/07	12/19/07	92
Douglas W. Webster	Chief Financial Officer	09/27/07	12/19/07	83
Neil Romano	Asst. Secy. – Disability Employment Policy	12/03/07	03/12/08	100
Alexander Passantino	Administrator – Wage and Hour Division	03/05/08	Returned 01/02/09a	
Brent R. Orrell	Asst. Secy. – Employment and Training Administration	06/19/08	Returned 01/02/09a	
Mean number of days to confirm a nomination			97	
Median number of days to confirm a nomination			92	

a. Returned to the President at the end of the 110th Congress under the provisions of Senate Rule XXXI, paragraph 6 of the Standing Rules of the Senate.

DEPARTMENT OF STATE (DOS)

Full-Time PAS Positions, as of the End of the 110th Congress.

Position[a]	Incumbent	Pay Level
Secretary	Condoleezza Rice	I
Deputy Secretary	John D. Negroponte	II
Deputy Secretary – Management and Resources[b]	Vacant	II
Under Secretary – Arms Control and International Security	John C. Rood (A)	III
Under Secretary – Economic, Business, and Agricultural Affairs	Reuben Jeffrey III	III
Under Secretary – Democracy and Global Affairs	Paula J. Dobriansky	III
Under Secretary – Management	Patrick F. Kennedy	III
Under Secretary – Political Affairs	William J. Burns	III
Under Secretary – Public Diplomacy and Public Affairs	James K. Glassman	III
Ambassador-at-Large – International Religious Freedom	John V. Hanford III	III
Inspector General[c]	Howard W. Geisel (A)	c
Ambassador-at-Large/Director – Office to Monitor and Combat Trafficking in Persons	Mark P. Lagon	IV
Ambassador-at-Large – War Crimes Issues	J. Clint Williamson	IV
Ambassador-at-Large/Coordinator – Counterterrorism	Dell L. Dailey	IV
Coordinator – U.S. Global AIDS	Mark R. Dybul	IV
Chief of Protocol	Nancy G. Brinker	IV
Assistant Secretary – Administration	Rajkumar Chellaraj	IV
Assistant Secretary – African Affairs	Jendayi E. Frazer	IV
Assistant Secretary – Consular Affairs	Janice L. Jacobs	IV
Assistant Secretary – Democracy, Human Rights, and Labor	David J. Kramer	IV
Assistant Secretary – Diplomatic Security/Director – Office of Foreign Missions[d]	Eric J. Boswell	IV
Assistant Secretary – East Asian and Pacific Affairs	Christopher R. Hill	IV
Assistant Secretary – Economic, Energy and Business Affairs	Daniel S. Sullivan	IV

Full-Time PAS Positions, as of the End of the 110th Congress (Continued).

Position[a]	Incumbent	Pay Level
Assistant Secretary – Educational and Cultural Affairs	Goli Ameri	IV
Assistant Secretary – European and Eurasian Affairs	Daniel Fried	IV
Assistant Secretary – Intelligence and Research	Randall M. Fort	IV
Assistant Secretary – International Narcotics and Law	David T. Johnson	IV
Enforcement Affairs		
Assistant Secretary – International Information Programs	Vacant	IV
Assistant Secretary – International Organization Affairs	Brian H. Hook	IV
Assistant Secretary – International Security and Nonproliferation	John C. Rood	IV
Assistant Secretary – Legislative Affairs	Matthew A. Reynolds	IV
Assistant Secretary – Near Eastern Affairs	C. David Welch	IV
Assistant Secretary – Oceans and International Environmental and Scientific Affairs	Claudia A. McMurray	IV
Assistant Secretary – Political-Military Affairs	Mark Kimmitt	IV
Assistant Secretary – Population, Refugees, and Migration Affairs	Vacant	IV
Assistant Secretary – Public Affairs	Sean I. McCormack	IV
Assistant Secretary – Resource Management/Chief Financial Officer[c]	Bradford R. Higgins	IV
Assistant Secretary – South and Central Asian Affairs	Richard A. Boucher	IV
Assistant Secretary – Verification, Compliance, and Implementation	Paula A. DeSutter	IV
Assistant Secretary – Western Hemisphere Affairs	Thomas A. Shannon Jr.	IV
Director General – Foreign Service [f]	Harry K. Thomas Jr.	IV
Legal Adviser International Organizations	John B. Bellinger III	IV
U.S. Representative – United Nations (U.N.)	Zalmay Khalilzad	II
U.S. Representative – Organization of American States	Hector E. Morales	[g]
U.S. Deputy Representative – U.N.	Alejandro D. Wolff	III
U.S. Representative – Economic and Social Council – U.N.	T. Vance McMahan	IV
U.S. Representative – Management and Reform – U.N.	Vacant	IV

Position[a]	Incumbent	Pay Level
U.S. Alternative Representative – Special Political Affairs – U.N.	Rosemary A. DiCarlo	IV

a The positions in this column do not include chiefs of mission in overseas posts or Foreign Service officers. In addition, certain officers of the State Department may be required to have certain qualifications. See 22 USCS § 2651a(g).

b The position of Deputy Secretary – Management and Resources in the Department of State was established by P.L. 106-553, § 404(a) (114 Stat. 2762A-96), enacted December 21, 2000. As of the end of the 110th Congress, this position had never been filled.

c The President may remove an inspector general (IG) from office, as he may remove most other appointed officials in the departments. In the case of an IG, however, the law provides that "[i]f an Inspector General is removed from office or is transferred to another position or location within an establishment, the President shall communicate in writing the reasons for any such removal or transfer to both Houses of Congress, not later than 30 days before the removal or transfer." (5 U.S.C. Appx. § 3 (b)). Under the provisions of 5 U.S.C. Appx. § 3 (e), "The annual rate of basic pay for an inspector general (as defined under section 12(3)) shall be the rate payable for level III of the Executive Schedule under section 5314 of title 5, United States Code, plus 3 percent."

d From 1998 through the end of the 110th Congress, each time an individual has been nominated to and confirmed for the position of Assistant Secretary for Diplomatic Security, he has simultaneously been nominated to and confirmed for the position of Director of Foreign Missions.

e The chief financial officer (CFO) may be appointed by the President, with the advice and consent of the Senate, or may be designated by the President from among agency officials who have been confirmed by the Senate for other positions (31 U.S.C. § 901(a)(1)). With regard to State Department appointments, since 2001 through the 110th Congress, the same individual had been separately and simultaneously nominated for, and confirmed to, the positions of CFO and Assistant Secretary for Resource Management.

f By law, incumbent must be a current or former career senior Foreign Service officer (22 U.S.C. § 3928).

g The salary for the U.S. Representative to the Organization of American States is linked to the pay for Chiefs of Mission. For this particular mission/ambassador, the salary is set based on the Executive Schedule Level III.

DOS Nomination Action During the 110th Congress.

Nominee	Position	Nominated	Confirmed	Days to Confirm
Ellen R. Sauerbrey	Asst. Secy. – Population, Refugees, and Migration	01/09/07	Returned 01/02/09[a]	
John D. Negroponte	Deputy Secy.	01/22/07	02/12/07	21
Zalmay Khalilzad	U.S. Representative – U.N.	02/12/07	03/29/07	45
Henry Bonilla	U.S. Representative – Organization of American States	03/15/07	Withdrawn 06/05/07	
Dell L. Dailey	Coordinator – Counterterrorism/ Ambassador-at-Large	03/15/07	06/22/07	99
Mark P. Lagon	Director – Office to Monitor and Combat Trafficking/Ambassador-at-Large[b]	03/15/07	05/25/07	71
John C. Rood	Under Secy. – Arms Control and International Security	03/22/07	Returned 01/02/09a	
Reuben Jeffrey III	Under Secy. – Economic, Business, and Agricultural Affairs	04/18/07	06/22/07	65
Nancy G. Brinker	Chief of Protocol	06/18/07	09/12/07	86
Mark Kimmitt	Asst. Secy. – Political-Military Affairs	07/11/07	06/27/08	352
David T. Johnson	Asst. Secy. – International Narcotics and Law Enforcement Affairs	07/19/07	10/26/07	99
Harry K. Thomas Jr.	Director General – Foreign Service	07/25/07	09/12/07	49
Patrick F. Kennedy	Under Secy. – Management	10/16/07	11/06/07	21
Goli Ameri	Asst. Secy. – Educational and Cultural Affairs	11/15/07	03/13/08	119

Nominee	Position	Nominated	Confirmed	Days to Confirm
Hector E. Morales	U.S. Representative – Organization of American States	12/04/07	03/06/08	93
James K. Glassman	Under Secy. – Public Diplomacy[b]	12/11/07	06/04/08	176
David J. Kramer	Asst. Secy. – Democracy, Human Rights, and Labor	12/14/07	03/13/08	90
T. Vance McMahan	U.S. Representative – Economic and Social Council – U.N.	03/13/08	06/27/08	106
William J. Burns	Under Secy. – Political Affairs	04/02/08	05/08/08	36
Janice L. Jacobs	Asst. Secy. – Consular Affairs	04/02/08	06/04/08	63
Eric J. Boswell	Asst. Secy. – Diplomatic Security/Director – Office of Foreign Missions	04/29/08	06/27/08	59
Rosemary A. DiCarlo	U.S. Alternative Representative – Special Political Affairs – U.N.	05/13/08	06/27/08	45
Matthew A. Reynolds	Asst. Secy. – Legislative Affairs	06/26/08	10/02/08	98
Thomas A. Betro	Inspector General	06/27/08	Returned 01/02/09a	
Brian H. Hook	Asst. Secy. – International Organization Affairs	06/27/08	10/02/08	97
Gregori Lebedev	U.S. Representative – Management and Reform – U.N.	08/01/08	Returned 01/02/09a	
Michael S. Doran	Asst. Secy. – International Information Programs	09/26/08	Returned 01/02/09a	
Mean number of days to confirm a nomination				90
Median number of days to confirm a nomination				86

a Returned to the President at the end of the 110th Congress under the provisions of Senate Rule XXXI, paragraph 6 of the Standing Rules of the Senate.

b As noted in the text of this report, position titles occasionally differ across the two tables provided for each department. In the State Department, the Director of the Office to Monitor and Combat Trafficking in Persons (listed in the incumbents table above) is the same position as the Office to Monitor and Combat Trafficking listed in this nomination table. The Under Secretary for Public Diplomacy and Public Affairs (listed in the incumbents table above) is the same position as the Under Secretary for Public Diplomacy listed here.

Department of Transportation (DOT)

Full-Time PAS Positions, as of the End of the 110th Congress.

Position	Incumbent	Pay Level
Secretary	Mary E. Peters	I
Deputy Secretary	Thomas J. Barrett	II
Under Secretary – Policy	Tyler D. Duvall (A)	II
Administrator – Federal Aviation Administration[a]	Robert A. Sturgell (A)	II
Administrator – Federal Highway Administration	Thomas J. Madison Jr.	II
Administrator – Federal Motor Carrier Safety Administration	John H. Hill	III
Administrator – Federal Railroad Administration	Vacant	III
Administrator – Federal Transit Administration	Vacant	III
Administrator – Maritime Administration	Sean T. Connaughton	III
Administrator – National Highway Traffic Safety Administration	Vacant	III
Administrator – Pipeline and Hazardous Materials Safety Administration	Carl T. Johnson	III
Administrator – Research and Innovative Technology Administration	Paul R. Brubaker	III
Inspector General[b]	Calvin L. Scovel	b
Administrator – Saint Lawrence Seaway Development Corporation[c]	Collister Johnson Jr.	IV
Assistant Secretary – Aviation and International Affairs	Michael W. Reynolds (A)	IV
Assistant Secretary – Budget and Programs/Chief Financial Officer[d]	Phyllis F. Scheinberg	IV
Assistant Secretary – Governmental Affairs	Vacant	IV
Assistant Secretary – Transportation Policy	Tyler D. Duvall	IV
Deputy Administrator – Federal Aviation Administration[e]	Ruth Leverentz (A)	IV
General Counsel	David J. Gribbin IV	IV

a This position has a five-year term and specified qualifications. See 49 U.S.C. § 106.

b The President may remove an inspector general (IG) from office, as he may remove most other appointed officials in the departments. In the case of an IG, however, the law provides that "[i]f an Inspector General is removed from office or is transferred to another position or location within an establishment, the President shall communicate in writing the reasons for any such removal or transfer to both Houses of Congress, not later than 30 days before the removal or transfer." (5 U.S.C. Appx. § 3 (b)). Under the provisions of 5 U.S.C. Appx. § 3 (e), "The annual rate of basic pay for an inspector general (as defined under section 12(3)) shall be the rate payable for level III of the Executive Schedule under section 5314 of title 5, United States Code, plus 3 percent."

c This position has a seven-year term. See 33 U.S.C. § 982(a).

d The chief financial officer (CFO) may be appointed by the President, with the advice and consent of the Senate, or may be designated by the President from among agency officials who have been confirmed by the Senate for other positions (31 U.S.C. § 901(a)(1)). Scheinberg was confirmed as Assistant Secretary for Budget and Programs and designated to serve as CFO.

e This position has specified qualifications. See 49 U.S.C. § 106.

DOT Nomination Action During the 110th Congress.

Nominee	Position	Nominated	Confirmed	Days to Confirm
David J. Gribbin IV	General Counsel	01/11/07	06/20/07	160
Thomas J. Barrett	Deputy Secy.	06/11/07	08/08/07	58
Paul R. Brubaker	Admin. – Research and Innovative Technology Administration	06/18/07	08/03/07	46
Simon C. Gros	Asst. Secy. – Governmental Affairs	10/16/07	06/27/08	255
Robert A. Sturgell	Admin. – Federal Aviation Administration	10/23/07	Returned 01/02/09[a]	
Carl T. Johnson	Admin. – Pipeline and Hazardous Materials Safety Administration	11/01/07	12/19/07	48
Tyler D. Duvall	Under Secy. – Policy	03/31/08	Returned 01/02/09[a]	
John P. Hewko	Asst. Secy. – Aviation and International Affairs	04/02/08	Returned 01/02/09[a]	
Thomas J. Madison Jr.	Admin. – Federal Highway Administration	07/15/08	08/01/08	17
David Kelly	Admin. – National Highway Traffic Safety Administration	09/28/08	Returned 01/02/09[a]	
Robert A. DeHaan	Asst. Secy. – Transportation Policy	11/17/08	Returned 01/02/09[a]	
Mean number of days to confirm a nomination			97	
Median number of days to confirm a nomination			53	

a. Returned to the President at the end of the 110th Congress under the provisions of Senate Rule XXXI, paragraph 6 of the Standing Rules of the Senate.

Department of the Treasury (TREAS)

Full-Time PAS Positions, as of the End of the 110th Congress.

Position	Incumbent	Pay Level
Secretary	Henry M. Paulson Jr.	I
Deputy Secretary	Robert M. Kimmitt	II
Commissioner of Internal Revenue[a]	Douglas H. Shulman	III
Comptroller of the Currency[b]	John C. Dugan	III
Director – Office of Thrift Supervision[c]	John M. Reich	III
Inspector General[d]	Eric M. Thorson	[d]
Inspector General – Tax Administration[d]	J. Russell George	[d]
Special Inspector General – Troubled Asset Relief Programde	Neil M. Barofsky	[d]
Under Secretary – Domestic Finance	Anthony W. Ryan (A)	III
Under Secretary – Terrorism and Financial Intelligence[f]	Stuart A. Levey	III
Under Secretary – International Affairs	David H. McCormick	III
Assistant Secretary – Economic Policy	Phillip L. Swagel	IV
Assistant Secretary – Financial Institutions	David G. Nason	IV
Assistant Secretary – Financial Markets	Karthik Ramanathan (A)	IV
Assistant Secretary – Intelligence and Analysis	Janice B. Gardner	IV
Assistant Secretary – International Economics and Development/Assistant Secretary (Interim) – Financial Stability[g]	Neel T. Kashkari	IV
Assistant Secretary – Management/Chief Financial Officer [h]	Peter B. McCarthy	IV
Assistant Secretary – Public Affairs	Michele A. Davis	IV
Assistant Secretary – Tax Policy	Eric Solomon	IV
Assistant Secretary – Terrorist Financing	Patrick M. O'Brien	IV
Assistant Secretary – International Affairs[i]	Clay Lowery	IV
Assistant Secretary – Legislative Affairs[i]	Kevin I. Fromer	IV
General Counsel	Robert F. Hoyt	IV
Chief Counsel – Internal Revenue Service/Assistant General Counsel for Tax	Donald L. Korb	V
Director of the Mint[j]	Edmund C. Moy	SL[k]
Treasurer of the United States	Anna E. Cabral	SL[k]

a This position has a five-year term and specified qualifications. See 26 U.S.C. § 7803(a)(1).

b This position has a five-year term, and a limitation on the President's removal power. See 12 U.S.C. § 2.

c This position has a five-year term and specified qualifications. See 12 U.S.C. § 1462a(c).

d The President may remove an inspector general (IG) from office, as he may remove most other appointed officials in the departments. In the case of an IG, however, the law provides that "[i]f an Inspector General is removed from office or is transferred to another position or location within an establishment, the President shall communicate in writing the reasons for any such removal or transfer to both Houses of Congress, not later than 30 days before the removal or transfer." (5 U.S.C. Appx. § 3 (b)). Under the provisions of 5 U.S.C. Appx. § 3 (e), "The annual rate of basic pay for an inspector general (as defined under section 12(3)) shall be the rate payable for level III of the Executive Schedule under section 5314 of title 5, United States Code, plus 3 percent."

e The position of Special Inspector General for the Troubled Asset Relief Program was established by P.L. 110- 343, Division A, Title 1, § 121, (122 Stat.3788). The position was first filled in the 110th Congress as shown. The Special Inspector General has the same removal provisions as other inspectors general (see footnote d, above).

f The position of Under Secretary for Terrorism and Financial Crimes (called Under Secretary for Terrorism and Financial Intelligence) was established by P.L. 108-447, Division H, Title II, § 222 (118 Stat. 3242). The Under Secretary was the successor office to the Office of Enforcement, and the incumbent in that office, Stuart A. Levey, continued to serve.

g The position of Interim Assistant Secretary for Financial Stability was established by P.L. 110-343, Division A, Title I, § 101(a)(3)(A), (122 Stat. 3767). The position was first filled in the 110th Congress as shown.

h The chief financial officer (CFO) may be appointed by the President, with the advice and consent of the Senate, or may be designated by the President from among agency officials who have been confirmed by the Senate for other positions (31 U.S.C. § 901(a)(1)). McCarthy was confirmed for the position of Assistant Secretary for Management and designated as CFO.

i The U.S. Code provides that the department has two deputy under secretaries appointed by the President with the advice and consent of the Senate. "When appointing each Deputy Under Secretary, the President may designate the Deputy Under Secretary as an Assistant Secretary" (31 U.S.C. § 301(d)). In each of these two cases, the President did so.

j The position has a five-year term and a limitation on the President's removal power. See 31 U.S.C. § 304.

k According to the 2008 Plum Book, the Director of the United States Mint and the Treasurer of the United States were both Senior Level positions (p. 132). With regard to pay for such positions, the Plum Book states, "Pay for SL [Senior Level] positions ranges from 120 percent of the rate of basic pay for GS-15, step 1 to the rate payable for level IV of the Executive Schedule. ... SL employees are entitled to locality-based comparability payments for their respective locality pay area. The employee's locality rate of pay may not exceed the pay for level III of the Executive Schedule" (p.203). See also 5 U.S.C. 5376 and 5 U.S.C. 5304(g)(2).

TREAS Nomination Action During the 110th Congress.

Nominee	Position	Nominated	Confirmed	Days to Confirm
David G. Nason	Asst. Secy. – Financial Institutions	03/05/07	06/05/07	92
Peter B. McCarthy	Asst. Secy. – Management	04/10/07	08/01/07	113
David H. McCormick	Under Secy. – International Affairs	06/04/07	08/01/07	58
Neel T. Kashkari	Asst. Secy. – International Economics and Development/Asst. Secy. (Interim) – Financial Stability	11/15/07	06/27/08	225
Eric M. Thorson	Inspector General	11/15/07	08/01/08	260
Douglas H. Shulman	Commissioner – Internal Revenue	12/11/07	03/13/08	93
Anthony W. Ryan	Under Secy. – Domestic Finance	07/31/08	Returned 01/02/09[a]	
Neil M. Barofsky	Special Inspector General – Troubled Asset Relief Program	11/17/08	12/08/08	21
Mean number of days to confirm a nomination				123
Median number of days to confirm a nomination				93

a. Returned to the President at the end of the 110th Congress under the provisions of Senate Rule XXXI, paragraph 6 of the Standing Rules of the Senate.

Department of Veterans Affairs (DVA)

Full-Time PAS Positions, as of the End of the 110th Congress.

Position	Incumbent	Pay Level
Secretary	James B. Peake	I
Deputy Secretary	Gordon H. Mansfield	II
Inspector Generala	George J. Opfer	a
Under Secretary – Benefits	Patrick W. Dunne	III
Under Secretary – Health	Michael J. Kussman	III
Under Secretary – Memorial Affairs	William F. Tuerk	III
Position	Incumbent	Pay Level
Assistant Secretary – Congressional and Legislative Affairs	Christine O. Hill	IV
Assistant Secretary – Human Resources and Administration	Vacant	IV
Assistant Secretary – Information and Technology	Robert T. Howard	IV
Assistant Secretary – Management/Chief Financial Officer[b]	Robert J. Henke	IV
Assistant Secretary – Operations, Preparedness, Security, and Law Enforcement[c]	Charles L. Hopkins	IV
Assistant Secretary – Policy and Planning	Karen Pane (A)	IV
Assistant Secretary – Public and Intergovernmental Affairs	Lisette M. Mondello	IV
Chairman – Board of Veterans' Appeals[d]	James P. Terry	IV
General Counsel	John A. Thompson (A)	IV

a The President may remove an inspector general (IG) from office, as he may remove most other appointed officials in the departments. In the case of an IG, however, the law provides that "[i]f an Inspector General is removed from office or is transferred to another position or location within an establishment, the President shall communicate in writing the reasons for any such removal or transfer to both Houses of Congress, not later than 30 days before the removal or transfer." (5 U.S.C. Appx. § 3 (b)). Under the provisions of 5 U.S.C. Appx. § 3 (e), "The annual rate of basic pay for an inspector general (as defined under section 12(3)) shall be the rate payable for level III of the Executive Schedule under section 5314 of title 5, United States Code, plus 3 percent."

b The chief financial officer (CFO) may be appointed by the President, with the advice and consent of the Senate, or may be designated by the President from among agency officials who have been confirmed by the Senate for other positions (31 U.S.C. § 901(a)(1)). Henke was confirmed for the position of Assistant Secretary for Management and designated as CFO.

c The position of Assistant Secretary for Operations, Preparedness, Security, and Law Enforcement was established by P.L. 107-287, Section 5 (116 Stat. 2030), and filled for the first time during the 110th Congress, as shown.

d This position has a six-year term and limitations on the President's removal power. See 38 U.S.C. § 7101(b).

DVA Nomination Action During the 110th Congress.

Nominee	Position	Nominated	Confirmed	Days to Confirm
Thomas E. Harvey	Asst. Secy. – Congressional Affairs[a]	01/09/07	05/25/07	136
Michael J. Kussman	Under Secy. – Health	04/10/07	05/25/07	45
Charles L. Hopkins	Asst. Secy. – Operations, Preparedness, Security and Law Enforcement	04/11/07	08/01/07	112
Paul J. Hutter	General Counsel	06/28/07	10/04/07	98
Michael W. Hager	Asst. Secy. – Human Resources and Management[a]	09/18/07	11/16/07	59
James B. Peake	Secretary	11/15/07	12/14/07	29
Christine O. Hill	Asst. Secy. – Congressional Affairs[a]	04/23/08	10/02/08	162
Patrick W. Dunne	Under Secy. – Benefits	07/30/08	10/02/08	64
Mean number of days to confirm a nomination				88
Median number of days to confirm a nomination				81

a. As noted in the text of this report, position titles occasionally differ across the two tables provided for each department. In the Veterans Affairs Department, the Assistant Secretary for Congressional and Legislative Affairs (listed in the incumbents table above) is the same position as the Assistant Secretary for Congressional Affairs listed in this nomination table. The Assistant Secretary for Human Resources and Administration (listed in the incumbents table above) is the same position as the Assistant Secretary for Human Resources and Management listed here.

APPENDIX A. PRESIDENTIAL NOMINATIONS, 110TH CONGRESS.

Nominee	Position	Department	Nomination Date	Confirmation Date	Days to Confirm
Clarence H. Albright Jr.	Under Secy.	DOE	06/21/07	08/03/07	43
Goli Ameri	Asst. Secy. – Education and Cultural Affairs	DOS	11/15/07	03/13/08	119
Carl Joseph Artman	Asst. Secy.	DOI	01/09/07	03/05/07	55
Neil M. Barofsky	Special Inspector General – Troubled Asset Relief Program	TREAS	11/17/08	12/08/08	21
Thomas J. Barrett	Deputy Secy.	DOT	06/11/07	08/08/07	58
Grace C. Becker	Asst. Atty. General – Civil Rights Division	DOJ	11/15/07	Returned 01/02/09	
Joseph A. Benkert	Asst. Secy. – International Security Policy	DOD	02/25/08	07/23/08 149	
Thomas A. Betro	Inspector General	DOS	06/27/08	Returned 01/02/09	
Anita K. Blair	Asst. Secy. – Air Force – Manpower and Reserve Affairs	DOD	01/09/07	Withdrawn 09/18/07	
Anita K. Blair	Asst. Secy. – Navy – Manpower and Reserve Affairs	DOD	09/18/07	Returned 12/31/07	
Anita K. Blair	Asst. Secy. – Navy – Manpower and Reserve Affairs	DOD	01/23/08	Returned 01/02/09	
Henry Bonilla	U.S. Representative – Organization of American States	DOS	03/15/07	Withdrawn 06/05/07	
Eric J. Boswell	Asst. Secy. – Diplomatic Security/Director – Office of Foreign Missions	DOS	04/29/08	06/27/08	59

Appendix A. (Continued).

Nominee	Position	Department	Nomination Date	Confirmation Date	Days to Confirm
Steven G. Bradbury	Asst. Atty. General – Office of Legal Counsel	DOJ	01/09/07	Returned 12/31/07	
Steven G. Bradbury	Asst. Atty. General – Office of Legal Counsel	DOJ	01/23/08	Returned 01/02/09	
William J. Brennan	Asst. Secy. – Oceans and Atmosphere	DOC	01/22/08	06/4/08	134
Jerry G. Bridges	Inspector General	ED	09/09/08	Returned 01/02/09	
Kerri L. Briggs	Asst. Secy. – Elementary and Secondary Education	ED	03/07/07	06/22/07	107
Nancy G. Brinker	Chief of Protocol	DOS	06/18/07	09/12/07	86
Douglas A. Brook	Asst. Secy. – Navy – Financial Management/Comptroller	DOD	06/05/07	11/16/07	164
Paul R. Brubaker	Admin. – Research and Innovative Technology Administration	DOT	06/18/07	08/03/07	46
Michael J. Burns	Asst. to the Secretary – Nuclear and Chemical and Biological Defense Programs	DOD	01/09/07	Withdrawn 06/11/07	
William J. Burns	Under Secy. – Political Affairs	DOS	04/02/08	05/08/08	36
Gregory B. Cade	Admin. – U.S. Fire Administration	DHS	01/09/07	05/25/07	136
Bradford P. Campbell	Asst. Secy. – Employee Benefits Security Administration	DOL	05/03/07	08/03/07	92
S. Ward Casscells	Asst. Secy. – Health Affairs	DOD	02/26/07	03/29/07	31

Nominee	Position	Department	Nomination Date	Confirmation Date	Days to Confirm
James L. Caswell	Dir. – Bureau of Land Management	DOI	06/04/07	08/03/07	60
Frederick S. Celec	Asst. to the Secretary – Nuclear and Chemical and Biological Defense Programs	DOD	06/10/08	07/23/08	43
Lily F. Claffee	General Counsel	DOC	03/31/08	06/04/08	65
James R. Clapper Jr.	Under Secy. – Intelligence	DOD	01/29/07	04/11/07	72
Gus P. Coldebella	General Counsel	DHS	10/16/07	Returned 01/02/09	
Elisebeth C. Cook	Asst. Atty. General – Office of Legal Policy	DOJ	01/30/08	06/04/08	126
J. Gregory Copeland	General Counsel	DOE	01/22/08	Withdrawn 06/24/08	
John Ray Correll	Dir. – Office of Surface Mining Reclamation and Enforcement	DOI	01/09/07	Withdrawn 06/28/07	
Robert M. Couch	General Counsel	HUD	04/10/07	06/13/07	64
Thomas P. D'Agostino	Under Secy. – Nuclear Security/Admin, NNSA	DOE	05/21/07	08/01/07	72
Dell L. Dailey	Coordinator – Counterterrorism	DOS	03/15/07	06/22/07	99
Paul DeCamp	Administrator – Wage and Hour Division	DOL	01/09/07	Withdrawn 02/07/08	
Robert A. DeHaan	Asst. Secy. – Transportation Policy	DOT	11/17/08	Returned 01/02/09	
Rosemary A. DiCarlo	U.S. Alternative Representative – Special Political Affairs – U.N.	DOS	05/13/08	06/27/08	45

Appendix A. (Continued).

Nominee	Position	Department	Nomination Date	Confirmation Date	Days to Confirm
Michael B. Donley	Secretary – Air Force	DOD	06/25/08	10/02/08	99
Michael S. Doran	Asst. Secy. – International Information Programs	DOS	09/26/08	Returned 01/02/09	
Craig W. Duehring	Asst. Secy. – Air Force – Manpower and Reserve Affairs	DOD	11/15/07	12/19/07	34
Elaine C. Duke	Under Secy. – Management	DHS	04/02/08	06/27/08	86
Patrick W. Dunne	Under Secy. – Benefits	DVA	07/30/08	10/02/08	64
Tyler D. Duvall	Under Secy. – Policy	DOT	03/31/08	Returned 01/02/09	
Cynthia Dyer	Dir. – Violence Against Women Office	DOJ	08/20/07	12/19/07	121
Lisa E. Epifani	Asst. Secy. – Congressional and Intergovernmental Affairs	DOE	06/13/07	08/03/07	51
Williamson Evers	Asst. Secy. – Planning, Evaluation, and Policy Development	ED	02/08/07	10/16/07	250
Mark R. Filip	Deputy Attorney General	DOJ	12/05/07	03/03/08	89
Nelson M. Ford	Under Secy. – Army	DOD	01/22/08	07/23/08	183
Matthew W. Friedrich	Asst. Atty. General – Criminal Division	DOJ	12/11/08	Returned 01/02/09	
Joxel Garcia	Asst. Secy. – Health	HHS	01/22/08	03/13/08	51

Nominee	Position	Department	Nomination Date	Confirmation Date	Days to Confirm
Regory G. Garre	Solicitor General	DOJ	06/19/08	10/02/08	105
Preston M. Geren	Secretary – Army	DOD	05/24/07	07/13/07	50
John H. Gibson	Asst. Secy. – Air Force – Financial Management/Comptroller	DOD	10/26/07	12/19/07	54
James K. Glassman	Under Secy. – Public Diplomacy	DOS	12/11/07	06/04/08	176
Sheila M. Greenwood	Asst. Secy. – Congressional and Intergovernmental Affairs	HUD	02/26/08	06/27/08	122
David J. Gribbin IV	General Counsel	DOT	01/11/07	06/20/07	160
Charles W. Grim	Director – Indian Health Service	HHS	05/21/07	Withdrawn 09/04/07	
Simon C. Gros	Asst. Secy. – Governmental Affairs	DOT	10/16/07	06/27/08	255
Michael W. Hager	Asst. Secy. – Human Resources and Management	DVA	09/18/07	11/16/07	59
David W. Hagy	Dir. – National Institute of Justice	DOJ	06/05/07	03/13/08	282
Keith Hall	Commissioner – Labor Statistics	DOL	09/18/07	12/19/07	92
Ondray T. Harris	Dir. – Community Relations Service	DOJ	05/23/07	03/13/08	295
Thomas E. Harvey	Asst. Secy. – Congressional Affairs	DVA	01/09/07	05/25/07	136
Robert Hastings	Asst. Secy. – Public Affairs	DOD	07/10/08	Returned 01/02/09	

Appendix A. (Continued).

Nominee	Position	Department	Nomination Date	Confirmation Date	Days to Confirm
John P. Hewko	Asst. Secy. – Aviation and International Affairs	DOT	04/02/08	Returned 01/02/09	
Christine O. Hill	Asst. Secy. – Congressional Affairs	DVA	04/23/08	10/02/08	162
Nathan J. Hochman	Asst. Atty. General – Tax Division	DOJ	11/15/07	12/19/07	34
James W. Holsinger Jr.	Surgeon General	HHS	05/24/07	Returned 01/02/09	
Brian H. Hook	Asst. Secy. – International Organization Affairs	DOS	06/27/08	10/02/08	97
Charles L. Hopkins	Asst. Secy. – Operations, Preparedness, Security and Law Enforcement	DVA	04/11/07	08/01/07	112
Paul J. Hutter	General Counsel	DVA	06/28/07	10/04/07	98
F. Chase Hutto, III	Asst. Secy. – International Affairs and Domestic Policy	DOE	09/26/08	Returned 01/02/09	
Steven J. Isakowitz	Chief Financial Officer	DOE	02/08/07	05/25/07	106
Gregory F. Jacob	Solicitor	DOL	09/04/07	12/19/07	106
Janice L. Jacobs	Asst. Secy. – Consular Affairs	DOS	04/02/08	06/04/08	63
David W. James	Asst. Secy. – Public Affairs	DOL	06/18/07	08/03/07	46
Robert D. Jamison	Under Secy. – National Protection and Programs	DHS	09/04/07	Withdrawn 12/19/07	

Nominee	Position	Department	Nomination Date	Confirmation Date	Days to Confirm
Robert D. Jamison	Under Secy. – National Protection and Programs	DHS	12/19/07	12/19/07	0
Reuben Jeffery III	Under Secy.– Economic, Business, and Agricultural Affairs	DOS	04/18/07	06/22/07	65
Harvey E. Johnson Jr.	Deputy Admin./ Chief Operating Officer – Federal Emergency Management Agency	DHS	09/07/07	Withdrawn 12/12/07	
Harvey E. Johnson Jr.	Deputy Admin./ Chief Operating Officer – Federal Emergency Management Agency	DHS	12/12/07	06/27/08	198
Carl T. Johnson	Admin. – Pipeline and Hazardous Materials Safety Administration	DOT	11/01/07	12/19/07	48
David T. Johnston	Asst. Secy. – International Narcotics and Law Enforcement Affairs	DOS	07/19/07	10/26/07	99
Diane A. Jones	Asst. Secy. – Postsecondary Education	ED	05/22/07	08/01/07	71
Tracy R. Justesen	Asst. Secy. – Special Education and Rehabilitative Services	ED	11/15/07	12/19/07	34
Neel T. Kashkari	Asst. Secy. – International Economics and Development/Asst. Secy. (Interim) – Financial Stability	TREAS	11/15/07	06/27/08	225
Gregory G. Katsas	Asst. Atty. General – Civil Division	DOJ	12/11/07	06/27/08	199
Scott A. Keller	Asst. Secy. – Congressional and Intergovernmental Affairs	HUD	01/09/07	Withdrawn 09/04/07	
David Kelly	Admin. – National Highway Traffic Safety Administration	DOT	09/28/08	Returned 01/02/09	
Patrick F. Kennedy	Under Secy. – Management	DOS	10/16/07	11/06/07	21
Zalmay Khalilzad	U.S. Representative – U.N.	DOS	02/12/07	03/29/07	45

Appendix A. (Continued).

Nominee	Position	Department	Nomination Date	Confirmation Date	Days to Confirm
Claude M. Kicklighter	Inspector General	DOD	02/26/07	04/12/07	45
Mark Kimmitt	Asst. Secy. – Political-Military Affairs	DOS	07/11/07	06/27/08	352
Kevin M. Kolevar	Asst. Secy. – Electricity Delivery and Energy Reliability	DOE	01/09/07	08/03/07	206
David J. Kramer	Asst. Secy. – Democracy, Human Rights, and Labor	DOS	12/14/07	03/13/08	90
Jeffery F. Kupfer	Deputy Secy.	DOE	04/02/08	Returned 01/02/09	
Michael K. Kussman	Under Secy. – Health	DVA	04/10/07	05/25/07	45
Holly A. Kuzmich	Asst. Secy. – Legislation and Congressional Affairs	ED	06/24/08	08/01/08	38
Mark P. Lagon	Director – Office to Monitor and Combat Trafficking	DOS	03/15/07	05/25/07	71
R. Lyle Laverty	Asst. Secy. – Fish and Wildlife	DOI	03/26/07	10/29/07	217
Gregori Lebedev	U.S. Representative – Management and Reform – U.N.	DOS	08/01/08	Returned 01/02/09	
Michele M. Leonhart	Admin. – Drug Enforcement	DOJ	04/15/08	Returned 01/02/09	
Mary Beth Long	Asst. Secy. – International Security Affairs	DOD	11/08/07	12/19/07	41
Jane C. Luxton	Asst. Secy. – Oceans and Atmosphere	DOC	01/09/07	Withdrawn 05/03/07	

Nominee	Position	Department	Nomination Date	Confirmation Date	Days to Confirm
Thomas J. Madison Jr.	Admin. – Federal Highway Administration	DOT	07/15/08	08/01/08	17
Mario Mancuso	Under Secy. – Export Administration	DOC	01/18/07	05/25/07	127
Christopher M. Marston	Asst. Secy. – Management	ED	06/24/08	08/01/08	38
Peter B. McCarthy	Asst. Secy. – Management	TREAS	04/10/07	08/01/07	113
David H. McCormick	Under Secy. – International Affairs	TREAS	06/04/07	08/01/07	58
T. Vance McMahan	U.S. Representative – Economic and Social Council – U.N.	DOS	03/13/08	06/27/08	106
Robert G. McSwain	Director – Indian Health Service	HHS	12/19/07	04/29/08	132
William W. Mercer	Associate Attorney General	DOJ	01/09/07	Withdrawn 06/25/07	
Daniel Meron	General Counsel	HHS	01/09/07	Returned 01/02/09	
Hector E. Morales	U.S. Representative – Organization of American States	DOS	12/04/07	03/06/08	93
Michael B. Mukasey	Attorney General	DOJ	09/21/07	11/08/07	48
Steven H. Murdock	Dir. - Census	DOC	06/18/07	12/19/07	184
Joseph J. Murin	President – Government National Mortgage Association	HUD	10/16/07	06/27/08	255
Julie L. Myers	Asst. Secy. – U.S. Immigration and Customs Enforcement	DHS	01/09/07	12/19/07	344

Appendix A. (Continued).

Nominee	Position	Department	Nomination Date	Confirmation Date	Days to Confirm
David G. Nason	Asst. Secy. – Financial Institutions	TREAS	03/05/07	06/05/07	92
John D. Negroponte	Deputy Secy.	DOS	01/22/07	02/12/07	21
Kevin J. O'Connor	Associate Attorney General	DOJ	12/11/07	04/01/08	112
Kameran L. Onley	Asst. Secy. – Water and Science	DOI	03/31/08	Returned 01/02/09	
Brent R. Orrell	Asst. Secy. – Employment and Training Administration	DOL	06/19/08	Returned 01/02/09	
William C. Ostendorff	Principal Deputy Administrator, NNSA	DOE	02/26/07	03/29/07	31
Christopher A. Padilla	Under Secy. – International Trade	DOC	09/04/07	12/19/07	106
Alexander Passantino	Administrator – Wage and Hour Division	DOL	03/05/08	Returned 01/02/09	
Neil S. Patel	Asst. Secy. – Communications and Information	DOC	03/05/08	Returned 01/02/09	
James B. Peake	Secretary	DVA	11/15/07	12/14/07	29
Christina H. Pearson	Asst. Secy. – Public Affairs	HHS	09/25/07	12/19/07	85
Susan D. Peppler	Asst. Secy. – Community Planning and Development	HUD	02/06/08	06/27/08	142
Steven C. Preston	Secretary	HUD	05/01/08	06/04/08	34

Nominee	Position	Department	Nomination Date	Confirmation Date	Days to Confirm
Howard Radzely	Deputy Secretary	DOL	05/10/07	12/19/07	223
Diane D. Rath	Asst. Secy. – Family Support	HHS	07/11/07	Returned 01/02/09	
Matthew A. Reynolds	Asst. Secy. – Legislative Affairs	DOS	06/26/08	10/02/08	98
Neil Romano	Asst. Secy. – Disability Employment Policy	DOL	12/03/07	03/12/08	100
John C. Rood	Under Secy. – Arms Control and International Security	DOS	03/22/07	Returned 01/02/09	
J. Patrick Rowan	Asst. Atty. General - National Security Division	DOJ	06/19/08	09/26/08	99
Jeffery W. Runge	Asst. Secy. – Health Affairs and Chief Medical Officer	DHS	08/02/07	12/19/07	139
Anthony W. Ryan	Under Secy. – Domestic Finance	TREAS	07/31/08	Returned 01/02/09	
Benjamin E. Sasse	Asst. Secy. – Planning and Evaluation	HHS	07/26/07	12/19/07	146
Ellen R. Sauerbrey	Asst. Secy. – Population, Refugees, and Migration	DOS	01/09/07	Returned 01/02/09	
Ed Schafer	Secretary	USDA	12/06/07	01/28/08	53
Jonathan R. Scharfen	Dir. – U.S. Citizenship and Immigration Services	DHS	10/01/08	Returned 01/02/09	
Paul A. Schneider	Deputy Secy.	DHS	02/26/08	06/04/08	99
Jeffrey L. Sedgwick	Asst. Atty. General – Office of Justice Programs	DOJ	04/23/08	10/02/08	162

Appendix A. (Continued).

Nominee	Position	Department	Nomination Date	Confirmation Date	Days to Confirm
Leon R. Sequeira	Asst. Secy. – Policy	DOL	01/09/07	02/15/07	37
Patrick P. Shen	Special Council for Immigration-Related Unfair Employment Practices	DOJ	01/18/07	10/04/07	259
James Shinn	Asst. Secy. – Asian and Pacific Security Affairs	DOD	10/23/07	12/19/07	57
Douglas H. Shulman	Commissioner – Internal Revenue	TREAS	12/11/07	03/13/08	93
James A. Slutz	Asst. Secy. – Fossil Energy	DOE	07/30/08	Returned 01/02/09	
Robert L. Smolen	Deputy Admin. – Defense Programs, NNSA	DOE	07/31/07	11/16/07	108
Sean J. Stackley	Asst. Secy. – Navy – Research, Development, and Acquisition	DOD	05/01/08	07/23/08	83
Richard Stickler	Asst. Secy. – Mine Safety and Health	DOL	01/09/07	Returned 01/02/09	
Robert A. Sturgell	Admin. – Federal Aviation Administration	DOT	10/23/07	Returned 01/02/09	
Stanley C. Suboleski	Asst. Secy. – Fossil Energy	DOE	12/11/07	Withdrawn 02/26/08	
John J. Sullivan	Deputy Secretary	DOC	12/04/07	03/13/08	100
Michael J. Sullivan	Dir. – Bureau of Alcohol, Tobacco, Firearms and Explosives	DOJ	03/22/07	Returned 01/02/09	
William G. Sutton Jr.	Asst. Secy. – Manufacturing and Services	DOC	05/07/07	08/03/07	88

Nominee	Position	Department	Nomination Date	Confirmation Date	Days to Confirm
Ronald J. Tenpas	Asst. Atty. General – Environment and Natural Resources Division	DOJ	06/04/07	12/13/07	192
Harry K. Thomas Jr.	Director General – Foreign Service	DOS	07/25/07	09/12/07	49
Eric M. Thorson	Inspector General	TREAS	11/15/07	08/01/08	260
Tevi D. Troy	Deputy Secy.	HHS	05/03/07	08/03/07	92
W. Craig Vanderwagen	Asst. Secy. – Preparedness and Response	HHS	02/12/07	03/21/07	37
Michael G. Vickers	Asst. Secy. – Special Operations and Low-Intensity Conflict	DOD	04/10/07	07/23/07	104
Brent T. Wahlquist	Dir. – Office of Surface Mining Reclamation and Enforcement	DOI	06/28/07	08/03/07	36
Christopher R. Wall	Asst. Secy. – Export Administration	DOC	03/31/08	06/27/08	88
Douglas W. Webster	Chief Financial Officer	DOL	09/27/07	12/19/07	83
John J. Young Jr.	Under Secy. – Acquisition, Technology and Logistics	DOD	06/21/07	11/16/07	11/16/07
Todd J. Zinser	Inspector General	DOC	09/07/07	12/19/07	103
Mean number of days to confirm				104	
Median number of days to confirm				92	

APPENDIX B. NOMINATION ACTION, 110TH CONGRESS.

Department	Positions	Nominations	Individual Nominees	Confirmations	Returned	Withdrawn	Mean Days to Confirm	Median Days to Confirm
Agriculture	16	1	1	1	0	0	53	53
Commerce	23	11	11	9	1	1	111	103
Defense	54	21	19	16	3	2	85	65
Education	18	7	7	6	1	0	90	55
Energy	22	12	12	7	3	2	88	72
Health and Human	20	10	10	6	3	1	91	89
Services								
Homeland Security	21	11	9	7	2	2	143	136
Housing and Urban	15	6	6	5	0	1	123	122
Development								
Interior	18	6	6	4	1	1	92	58
Justice	29	21	20	14	6	1	152	124
Labor	20	12	12	8	3	1	97	92
State	48	27	27	21	5	1	90	86
Transportation	20	11	11	6	5	0	97	53
Treasury	26	8	8	7	1	0	123	93
Veterans Affairs	15	8	8	8	0	0	88	81
Total	364	172	167	125	34	13	104	92

Note: Similar previous reports included a column in this table for recess appointments. Because President Bush did not make any recess appointments to executive departments during the 110th Congress, a recess appointments column is not included.

APPENDIX C. SENATE INTERSESSION RECESSES AND INTRASESSION RECESSES OF FOUR OR MORE DAYS, 110TH CONGRESS.

Date Recessed	Date Reconvened	Number of Days Adjournedb
(The first session of the 110th Congress convened on January 4, 2007.)		
02/17/07	02/26/07	9
03/29/07	04/10/07	12
05/25/07	06/04/07	10
06/29/07	07/09/07	10
08/03/07	09/04/07	32
10/05/07	10/15/07	10

The Senate adjourned sine die on December 31, 2007. The second session of the 110th Congress convened on January 3, 2008. The intersession (period between these two dates) was 3 days long.b There were no intrasession recesses of four or more days during the 110th Congress, 2nd session. The Senate adjourned its second session on January 2, 2009.

Source: Table created by the Congressional Research Service using data from the *Congressional Record.*

Note: For the purposes of determining the length of an intrasession recess for inclusion in this table, Sundays were not counted. Under congressional precedents, Sunday is considered a "dies non," or a day on which Congress is not expected to meet, for purposes of determining whether Congress has adjourned for "not more than three days."

b. The number of days adjourned was counted starting on the first calendar day after an adjournment and ending on the day of reconvening, including in the count the day the Senate reconvened. This is consistent with the House practice for counting recess days for the purposes of meeting congressional adjournment requirements in the Constitution ("Neither House, during the Session of Congress, shall, without the Consent of the other, adjourn for more than three days ...." Art. I, § 5, cl. 4). Under House precedents, "The House of Representatives in adjourning for not more than three days must take into the count either the day of adjourning or the day of the meeting, and Sunday is not taken into account in making this computation" U.S. Congress, House, *Constitution, Jefferson's Manual and Rules of the House of Representatives of the United States, One Hundred Tenth Congress*, 109th Cong., 2nd sess., H.Doc. 109-157 (Washington: GPO, 2007), p. 37. Senate practice appears to be consistent with this approach (Floyd M. Riddick and Alan S. Frumin, *Riddick's Senate Procedure: Precedents and Practices*, 101st Cong., 2nd sess., S.Doc. 101-28, (Washington: GPO, 1992), pp. 15-16). Inasmuch as it has been argued that the periods during which the President could make recess appointments might be those in which the Senate is in recess pursuant to the constitutional provision just quoted, it appears that this method of calculating recess days would provide a relevant measure of recess length in the context of discussions of recess appointments. Other methods might be used in other contexts. For example, a method in which neither the day of adjournment nor the day of reconvening was counted has been used elsewhere. This method takes into account that the Senate could act on nominations on either of these days, obviating the need for a recess appointment.

APPENDIX D. ABBREVIATIONS OF DEPARTMENTS

DHS	Department of Homeland Security
DOC	Department of Commerce
DOD	Department of Defense
DOE	Department of Energy
DOI	Department of the Interior
DOJ	Department of Justice
DOL	Department of Labor
DOS	Department of State
DOT	Department of Transportation
DVA	Department of Veterans Affairs
ED	Department of Education
HHS	Department of Health and Human Services
HUD	Department of Housing and Urban Development
TREAS	Department of the Treasury
USDA	Department of Agriculture

APPENDIX E. CHANGE IN METHODOLOGY FROM PREVIOUS TRACKING REPORTS

The calculations of nomination-to-confirmation intervals provided in this report counted all the days within the interval, including those during summer recesses and between sessions of the Senate. The inclusion of all days differs from the methodology used in similar CRS reports for previous Congresses.[34] In these earlier reports, days during August and intersession recesses were not included in calculations of nomination-to-confirmation intervals. The rationale for the earlier methodology was that the Senate was unlikely to continue consideration of nominations during these periods; committee hearings and votes, among other activities, typically do not occur during these times. The exclusion of days during only certain periods of adjournment—intersession recesses and August recesses, which are usually longer than 30 days—is suggested by Senate rules regarding when nominations are to be returned to the President. These provide,

> Nominations neither confirmed nor rejected during the session at which they are made shall not be acted upon at any succeeding session without being again made to the Senate by the President; and if the Senate shall adjourn or take recess for more than thirty days, all nominations pending and not finally acted upon at the time of taking such adjournment or recess shall be returned by the Secretary to the President. 35

This earlier methodology was also consistent with the approach of some political scientists who study executive branch appointments.[36]

The methodology for this report is different from that which was used in previous similar reports for several reasons. First, as discussed above in the section on recess appointments, from the latter part of the first session through the end of the 110th Congress, the Senate chose to break up what would otherwise have been longer recesses into shorter recesses separated by pro forma sessions. This introduced two options for this report with regard to the calculation of nomination-toconfirmation intervals. The first option would have been to treat each series of short recesses created in this fashion as one long recess and to subtract these days from the nomination-toconfirmation interval.[37] The second option would have been to treat each recess in the series of short recesses created in this fashion as a short recess, and not to subtract these days from the nomination-to-confirmation interval. Arguably, actions of the Senate and the President were consistent with the latter construction—short recesses as short recesses. Otherwise, Senate rules would have required the return of pending nominations (or the waiver of that rule)[38] and the President could have made recess appointments. The Senate and the President did not take these actions. As a result, short recesses created by pro forma sessions are treated as short recesses in the count of the length of time to confirmation. It should be noted, however, that the inclusion of these days reduces the comparability of statistics provided in this report with statistics in previous similar tracking reports, since the intervals calculated in this report include days that in previous reports were part of longer recesses and therefore were subtracted from the length of the interval. Although the phenomenon underlying this methodological problem first arose during the 110th Congress, it could arise again in future Congresses.

Other reasons for the methodological change are not unique to the 110th Congress. First, in some cases, committee or floor action on a nomination that could have been completed before a recess has been, instead, deferred until after the recess. For such a nomination, the period of Senate consideration arguably has been intentionally extended. Counting all days, including those during a long recess, in calculations of elapsed time reflects that extension of Senate consideration. Second, it is unlikely that all work pertaining to nominations stops over a recess, and the inclusion of recess days is a reflection of the fact that the nominee is still under consideration, even during recess. Member and committee staffs may still be considering nominations at that time, even though they may not take direct action in the form of hearings or votes on the nominees. Ongoing activities may include investigatory work and interviews with nominees. Finally, although, as mentioned above, some political scientists who study nominations do subtract recess days during calculations of nomination-to-confirmation intervals, many others do not.[39] In addition, the calculation of nomination-to-confirmation intervals in CRS research concerning judicial nominations does not exclude days that fall during recesses.[40] By using methodology that is more similar to the work of other political scientists and to CRS judicial nominations research, the research presented here could be more easily compared and combined with related work. For all of these reasons, in this report, we employ a new methodology for calculating nomination-to-confirmation intervals.

ACKNOWLEDGMENTS

Terrence L. Lisbeth, Reference Assistant, and Mabel Gracias, Library Technician Reference Assistant, assisted in the collection of data used in this report.

End Notes

[1] Full-time departmental PAS positions that are not covered in this report include U.S. attorney and U.S. marshal positions in the Department of Justice; most Foreign Service and diplomatic positions in the Department of State; officer corps positions in the civilian

uniformed services of the National Oceanic and Atmospheric Administration in the Department of Commerce, and of the Public Health Service in the Department of Health and Human Services; and the officer corps in the military services.

[2] A succinct historical and contemporary overview of the appointment power is found in Louis Fisher, "Appointment Powers," in his *Constitutional Conflicts between Congress and the President,* 5th ed., rev. (Lawrence, KS: University Press of Kansas, 2007), pp. 21-47.

[3] Art. II, Sec. 2, cl. 2 provides that the President "shall nominate, and by and with the Advice and Consent of the Senate, shall appoint Ambassadors, other public Ministers and Consuls, Judges of the supreme Court, and all other Officers of the United States, whose Appointments are not herein otherwise provided for, and which shall be established by Law: but the Congress may by Law vest the Appointment of such inferior Officers, as they think proper, in the President alone, in the Courts of Law, or in the Heads of Departments."

[4] The Council for Excellence in Government's Presidential Appointee Initiative, *A Survivor's Guide for Presidential Nominees*, The Brookings Institution, Washington, D.C., November 2000, pp. 31-32.

[5] See, for example, Michael J. Gerhardt, *The Federal Appointments Process: A Constitutional and Historical Analysis* (Durham: Duke University Press, 2003), pp. 29-34.

[6] See, for example, ibid., pp. 152-153.

[7] 3 U.S.C. § 102 note.

[8] P.L. 108-458, § 7601; 118 Stat. 3856.

[9] 5 U.S.C. § 3349a.

[10] P.L. 105-277, Div. C, Title I, § 151; 5 U.S.C. §§ 3345-3349d. For more on the Vacancies Act, see CRS Report 98-892, *The New Vacancies Act: Congress Acts to Protect the Senate's Confirmation Prerogative*, by Morton Rosenberg.

[11] For further information on this stage of the appointment process, see CRS Report RL31980, *Senate Consideration of Presidential Nominations: Committee and Floor Procedure*, by Elizabeth Rybicki; and CRS Report RL31948, *Evolution of the Senate's Role in the Nomination and Confirmation Process: A Brief History*, by Betsy Palmer.

[12] G. Calvin Mackenzie, *The Politics of Presidential Appointments* (New York: The Free Press, 1981), pp. 97-189.

[13] Formally, the presiding officer of the Senate makes the referrals. For more information, see Floyd M. Riddick and Alan S. Frumin, *Riddick's Senate Procedure: Precedents and Practices,* 101st Cong., 2nd sess., S.Doc. 101-28 (Washington: GPO, 1992), pp. 1154-8; and CRS Report RL31980, *Senate Consideration of Presidential Nominations: Committee and Floor Procedure*, by Elizabeth Rybicki, pp. 2-3.

[14] One example of such an occurrence was the Senate Judiciary Committee's rejection of William Lucas, whom President George H. W. Bush had nominated for Assistant Attorney General for Civil Rights. Reportedly, the committee first rejected reporting the nomination favorably, then the committee rejected sending the nomination to the full Senate without any recommendation. Although the disposition of the vote was 7-7, a majority is required to report a nomination out of committee. For further information on this example, see "Senate Panel Rejects Lucas for Rights Post," *St. Louis Post-Dispatch*, August 2, 1989, p. 1A.

[15] For more information, see CRS Report RL31980, *Senate Consideration of Presidential Nominations: Committee and Floor Procedure*, by Elizabeth Rybicki, p. 7.

[16] The rule may be found in U.S. Congress, Senate Committee on Rules and Administration, *Senate Manual*, 110th Cong., 2nd sess., S. Doc. 110-1 (Washington: GPO, 2008), p. 58, Rule XXXI, paragraph 6 of the Standing Rules of the Senate.

[17] For an example of a waiver of the rule, see Sen. Harry Reid, "Nominations Status Quo," *Congressional Record*, daily edition, vol. 153, December 19, 2007, p. S16061.

[18] Art. II, Sec. 2, cl. 3.

[19] 5 U.S.C. § 5503(a).

[20] 5 U.S.C. § 5503(b).

[21] For further information, see CRS Report RS21308, *Recess Appointments: Frequently Asked Questions*, by Henry B. Hogue; and CRS Report RL33009, *Recess Appointments: A Legal Overview*, by T. J. Halstead.

[22] 15 Op. O.L.C. 93 (1991). See also 6 Op. O.L.C. 585 (1982); 41 Op. A.G. 463 (1960).

[23] P.L. 110-161, Div. D, § 709.

[24] A pro forma session is a short meeting of the House or Senate during which it is understood that no business will be conducted.

[25] The Constitution does not specify how long the Senate must be in recess for the President to have the ability to make a recess appointment. The three-day norm derives from a Justice Department brief written in 1993. In this brief, the authors posited that because the Constitution allows the Senate to adjourn its session for up to three days without obtaining the consent of the House, a recess of three days or fewer is not considered "constitutionally significant." Over the past two decades, the shortest recess during which a President made an appointment was 10 days. For more information, see CRS Report RS21308, *Recess Appointments: Frequently Asked Questions*, by Henry B. Hogue. For the Justice Department brief, see *Mackie v. Clinton*, Memorandum of Points and Authorities in Support of Defendants' Opposition to Plaintiffs' Motion for Partial Summary Judgment, at 24-26, Civ. Action No. 93-0032-LFO, (D.D.C. 1993).

[26] For further information, see CRS Report RS21308, *Recess Appointments: Frequently Asked Questions*, by Henry B. Hogue.

[27] 5 U.S.C. §§ 3345-3349d.

[28] For more on the Vacancies Act, see CRS Report 98-892, *The New Vacancies Act: Congress Acts to Protect the Senate's Confirmation Prerogative*, by Morton Rosenberg.

[29] Senate Rule XXXI, paragraph 6 of the Standing Rules of the Senate provides that "Nominations neither confirmed not rejected during the session at which they are made shall not be acted upon at any succeeding session without being again made to the Senate by the President; and if the Senate shall adjourn or take a recess for more than thirty days, all nominations pending and not finally acted upon at the time of taking such adjournment or recess shall be returned by the Secretary to the President, and shall not again be considered unless they shall again be made to the Senate by the President." U.S. Congress, Senate Committee on Rules and Administration, *Senate Manual*, 110th Cong., 2nd sess., S. Doc. 110-1 (Washington: GPO, 2008), p. 58.

[30] Sources include the Senate nominations database of the Legislative Information System http://www.congress.gov/nomis/, the *Congressional Record* (daily edition), the *Weekly Compilation of Presidential Documents*, telephone discussions with agency officials, agency websites, the *United States Code*, and the 2008 "Plum Book" (U.S. Congress, Senate Committee on Homeland Security and Governmental Affairs, *United States Government Policy and Supporting Positions*, committee print, 110th Cong., 2nd sess., November 12, 2008, S. Prt. 110-36 (Washington: GPO, 2008)).

[31] The data collected on incumbents at the end of the 110th Congress were collected as of the Senate's last day of business on December 11, 2008. Beginning on December 12, agency officials were contacted and the lists of incumbents were finalized.

[32] As noted above, the following full-time positions are not included in this report: U.S. Attorney and U.S. Marshal positions in the Department of Justice; Foreign Service and diplomatic positions in the Department of State; most officer corps positions in the civilian uniformed services of the National Oceanic and Atmospheric Administration in the Department of Commerce, and of the Public Health Service in the Department of Health and Human Services; and the officer corps in the military services.

[33] In some cases, the title drawn from the LIS database is expanded upon for clarity in the second table. For example, Sheila M. Greenwood was nominated to be Assistant Secretary of Housing and Urban Development (HUD). Her nomination, as shown in the LIS database, does not indicate *which* Assistant Secretary position she was nominated to; it merely states that she was nominated as an Assistant Secretary. In the section on HUD, the second table shows that she was nominated to be Assistant Secretary for Congressional and Intergovernmental Affairs. The expansion of this title was based upon knowledge of the previous position holder and the title held by that individual. This information is included to give the reader a better understanding of the position to which the individual was nominated.

[34] See, for example, CRS Report RL34744, *Presidential Appointments to Full-Time Positions on Regulatory and Other Collegial Boards and Commissions, 109th Congress*, by Henry B. Hogue et al.

[35] U.S. Congress, Senate Committee on Rules and Administration, *Senate Manual*, 110th Cong., 2nd sess., S.Doc. 110-1 (Washington: GPO, 2008), p. 58, Rule XXXI, paragraph 6 of the Standing Rules of the Senate.

[36] For example, see Nolan McCarty and Rose Razaghian, "Advice and Consent: Senate Responses to Executive Branch Nominations 1885-1996," *American Journal of Political Science*, vol. 43, no. 4 (October 1999), pp. 1122-1143.

[37] This appears to be the construction adopted by the *Congressional Directory*. See U.S. Congress, Joint Committee on Printing, *Congressional Directory, 2009-2010,* 111th Cong., 1st sess., S. Pub. 111-14 (Washington: GPO, 2009), p. 541.

[38] As noted above, under Senate rules, if a nomination is not acted upon by the Senate by the end of a Congress, it is returned to the President. Pending nominations also may be returned automatically to the President at the beginning of a recess of more than 30 days, but the Senate rule providing for this return is often waived. The applicable Senate rule may be found in U.S. Congress, Senate Committee on Rules and Administration, *Senate Manual*, 110th Cong., 2nd sess., S. Doc. 110-1 (Washington: GPO, 2008), p. 58, Rule XXXI, paragraph 6 of the Standing Rules of the Senate.

[39] For example, see Lauren Cohen Bell, "Senatorial Discourtesy: The Senate's Use of Delay to Shape the Federal Judiciary," *Political Research Quarterly*, vol. 55, no. 3 (September 2002), pp. 589-607; Sarah A. Binder and Forrest Maltzman, "Senatorial Delay in Confirming Federal Judges, 1947-1998," *American Journal of Political Science*, vol. 46, no. 1 (January 2002), pp. 190-199; and Karl DeRouen Jr., Jeffrey S. Peake, and Kenneth Ward, "Presidential Mandates and the Dynamics of Senate Advice and Consent, 1885-1996," *American Politics Research*, vol. 33, no. 1 (January 2005), pp. 106-131.

[40] For example, see CRS Report RL33953, *Nominations to Article III Lower Courts by President George W. Bush During the 110th Congress*, by Denis Steven Rutkus, Susan Navarro Smelcer, and Maureen Bearden.

In: Presidential Appointments
Editors: C. P. Dempsey, J. L. Milford
ISBN: 978-1-61324-067-0

Chapter 2

PRESIDENTIAL APPOINTMENTS TO FULL-TIME POSITIONS ON REGULATORY AND OTHER COLLEGIAL BOARDS AND COMMISSIONS, 110TH CONGRESS*

Henry B. Hogue and Maureen Bearden

SUMMARY

The President makes appointments, with the advice and consent of the Senate, to some 152 full-time leadership positions on 34 federal regulatory and other collegial boards and commissions. This appointment process consists of three distinct stages: selection, clearance, and nomination by the President; consideration by the Senate; and appointment by the President. These advice and consent positions can also temporarily be filled by the President alone through a recess appointment. Membership positions on this set of collegial bodies often have fixed terms, and incumbents are often protected from arbitrary removal by the President. The enabling statutes for most of these boards and commissions require political party balance in their membership.

During the 110th Congress, President George W. Bush submitted nominations to the Senate for 74 of these 152 positions. (Most of the remaining positions on these boards and commissions were not vacant

---

* This is an edited, reformatted and augmented version of a Congressional Research Services publication, dated October 25, 2010.

during that time.) A total of 88 nominations were submitted, of which 46 were confirmed, 15 were withdrawn, and 27 were returned to the President. The number of nominations exceeded the number of positions because the President submitted multiple nominations for some positions. In some cases the President submitted one nomination for the end of a term in progress and a second nomination of the same person to the same position for the succeeding term. In other cases, the President submitted a second nomination after his first choice failed to be confirmed. President Bush made one recess appointment to a board covered by this report during the 110th Congress, and he submitted an "extra" nomination of that individual in order to comply with a law affecting the payment of that appointee. At the end of the 110th Congress, 15 incumbents were serving past the expiration of their terms. In addition, there were 22 vacancies among the 152 positions.

This report specifies, for the 110th Congress, all nominations to full-time positions on 34 regulatory and other collegial boards and commissions. Profiles of each board and commission provide information on their organizational structures, membership as of the end of the 110th Congress, and appointment activity during that Congress. The organizational section discusses the statutory requirements for the appointed positions, including the number of members on each board or commission, their terms of office, whether or not they may continue in their positions after their terms expire, whether or not political balance is required, and the method for selection of the chair. Membership and appointment activity are provided in tabular form. The report also includes tables summarizing the collective appointment activity for all 34 bodies, and identifying Senate recesses during the 110th Congress.

The calculations of nomination-to-confirmation intervals provided in this report counted all the days within the interval, including those during summer recesses and between sessions of the Senate. The inclusion of all days differs from the methodology used in similar CRS reports for previous Congresses. The new methodology takes into consideration changes in Senate adjournment practices and is consistent with published research in this area. This change may reduce the comparability of statistics in this report with those of the earlier research.

Information for this report was compiled from data from the Senate nominations database of the Legislative Information System at http://www.congress.gov/nomis/, telephone discussions with agency officials, agency websites, the United States Code, and the 2008 edition of *United States Government Policy and Supporting Positions* (more commonly known as the "Plum Book").

INTRODUCTION

This report provides an overview of the process for filling positions to which the President makes appointments with the advice and consent of the Senate (PAS positions). It also specifies, for the 110th Congress (January 2007-January 2009), all nominations to full-time positions on 34 regulatory and other collegial boards and commissions that have such positions (e.g., the Consumer Product Safety Commission, the Federal Reserve Board, and the Election Assistance Commission). Profiles of each board and commission provide information on their organizational structures, membership as of the end of the 110th Congress, and appointment activity during that Congress.

The Appointment Process for PAS Positions

The President and the Senate share the power to appoint the principal officers of the United States.[1] The Constitution (Article II, Section 2, clause 2) empowers the President to nominate and, by and with the advice and consent of the Senate, to appoint the principal officers of the United States.[2] Three distinct stages mark the appointment process: selection, clearance, and nomination by the President; consideration by the Senate; and appointment by the President.

Selection, Clearance, and Nomination

In this stage, the White House selects and clears a nominee before sending the formal nomination to the Senate. There are a number of steps in this stage of the process for most Senate-confirmed positions. First, with the assistance of, and preliminary vetting by, the White House Office of Presidential Personnel, the President selects a candidate for the position. Interested parties, including Members of Congress, often have input during this process. Most boards and commissions are required, by statute, to have a political balance among their members (i.e., no more than a simple majority may be from the same political party), so the President normally negotiates over nominations with leaders of the opposition party in Congress. These negotiations involve questions not only of patronage but of policy, especially when the board or commission is involved in areas that, at the time, may be particularly sensitive. This often results in a packaging process in which the President submits several nominations together for positions in a particular agency and the Senate then confirms them as a group. Sometimes, however, only one or two nominations are submitted when three or four positions may be available. When this occurs, a nomination may remain before the Senate for many months, until one or two additional nominations are submitted. Generally, all are then quickly confirmed.

During the clearance process, the candidate prepares and submits several forms: the "Public Financial Disclosure Report" (Standard Form (SF) 278), the "Questionnaire for National Security Positions" (SF 86), and the White House "Personal Data Statement Questionnaire." The Office of the Counsel to the President oversees the clearance process, which often includes background investigations conducted by the Federal Bureau of Investigation (FBI), the Internal Revenue Service (IRS), the Office of Government Ethics (OGE), and an ethics official for the agency to which the candidate is to be appointed. If conflicts are found during the background check, OGE and the agency ethics officer may work with the candidate to mitigate the conflicts. Once the Office of the Counsel to the President has cleared the candidate, the nomination is ready to be submitted to the Senate.

The selection and clearance stage is often the longest part of the appointment process. There can be lengthy delays, particularly if many candidates are being processed, as they are at the beginning of an Administration,[3] or if conflicts need to be resolved. Candidates for higher-level positions are often accorded priority in this process. In an effort to reduce the elapsed time between a new President's inauguration and the appointment of his or her national security team, provisions added in 2004 to the Presidential Transition Act of 1963 encourage Presidents-elect to submit, for security clearance, potential nominees to high-level national security positions as soon as possible after the election.[4]

For positions located within a state (e.g., U.S. attorneys, U.S. marshals, and U.S. district judges), the President, by custom, normally nominates an individual recommended by the Senator or Senators (if they are from the same party as the President) from that state.[5] If neither Senator is from the President's party, the President usually defers to the recommendations of party leaders from the state. Occasionally, the President solicits recommendations from Senators of the opposition party because of their positions in the Senate. Before making a nomination to a federal position at the state or national level, the President would consider how it will fare in the confirmation process.

A nominee has no legal authority to assume the duties and responsibilities of the position; the authority comes with Senate confirmation and presidential appointment. A nominee who is hired by the agency as a consultant while awaiting confirmation may serve only in an advisory capacity. If circumstances permit and conditions are met, the President may give the nominee a recess appointment to the position (see below). Recess appointments may have political consequences, however, particularly if Senators perceive that an appointment is an effort to circumvent their constitutional role. Some Senate-confirmed positions, such as many of those in the executive departments, may also be temporarily filled under the Federal Vacancies Reform Act of 1998.[6] Positions on most boards and commissions, however, are not covered by this act.[7]

Senate Consideration

In the confirmation or second stage, the Senate alone determines whether or not to confirm a nomination.[8] The way the Senate acts on a nomination depends largely on the importance of the position involved, existing political circumstances, and policy implications. Generally, the Senate shows particular interest in the nominee's views and how they are likely to affect public policy.[9] Two other factors may also affect the scrutiny with which a nominee's personal and professional qualities are examined: whether or not the President's party controls the Senate and the degree to which the President becomes involved in supporting the nomination.

The Senate confirmation process is centered at the committee level. On the day the President submits a nomination to the Senate, the Senate's executive clerk refers it to the appropriate committee or committees. When making a referral, the executive clerk is guided by Senate Rule XXV, which establishes the subject matters under the purview of each committee and directs that "all proposed legislation, messages, petitions, memorials, and other matters relating primarily to [those] subjects" be referred to that committee. The executive clerk is also guided by precedents set by prior referrals and by standing orders and unanimous consent (UC) agreements pertaining to referral of nominations.[10] Most nominations are sent to a single committee. Occasionally, the Senate has agreed, by unanimous consent, by standing order, or by statute, to refer one or more nominations to more than one committee.

Committee nomination activity generally includes investigation, hearing, and reporting stages. As part of investigatory work, committees may draw on information provided by the White House as well as information they themselves collect. Hearings provide a public forum to discuss a nomination and any issues related to the program or agency for which the nominee would be responsible. Even if confirmation is thought to be a virtual certainty, hearings may provide Senators and the nominee with an opportunity to go on the record with particular views or commitments. Senators may use hearings to explore a nominee's qualifications, articulate a policy perspective, or raise related oversight issues. Some committees hold hearings on nearly all nominations that are referred to them; others hold hearings for only some.

The committee may discontinue acting on a nomination at any point—upon referral, after investigation, or after a hearing. If the committee votes to report the nomination back to the full Senate, it has three options: it may report the nomination to the Senate favorably, report it unfavorably, or report it without recommendation. If the committee elects not to report a nomination, the Senate may, under certain circumstances, discharge the committee from further consideration of the nomination in order to bring it to the floor.[11]

Although the Senate confirms most nominations, some nominations are not confirmed. Rarely, however, does the full Senate reject a nomination. Most nominations that are not confirmed fail in committee, either by committee vote or by committee inaction. Rejections in committee occur for a variety of reasons, including opposition to the nomination, inadequate amount of time for consideration of the nomination, or factors that may have nothing to do with the merits of the nomination. If a nomination is not acted upon by the Senate by the end of a Congress, it is returned to the President. Pending nominations also may be returned automatically to the President at the beginning of a recess of more than 30 days, but the Senate rule providing for this return is often waived.[12]

Appointment

In the final stage, the confirmed nominee is given a commission signed by the President, with the seal of the United States affixed thereto, and is sworn into office. The President may sign the commission at any time after confirmation. Once the appointee is given the commission and sworn in, he or she has full authority to carry out the responsibilities of the office.

Recess Appointments

The Constitution also empowers the President to make limited-term appointments without Senate confirmation when the Senate is in recess.[13] Such recess appointments expire at the end of the next full session of the Senate. **Table B-1** provides the dates of the Senate recesses for the 110th Congress. One recess appointment was made to a position on a regulatory or other collegial board or commission during the 110th Congress for reasons discussed below. The recess during which this took place is shown in the table.[14]

Presidents have occasionally used the recess appointment power to circumvent the confirmation process. In response, Congress has placed restrictions on the President's authority to make a recess appointment. Under 5 U.S.C. § 5503(a), if the position to which the President makes a recess appointment falls vacant while the Senate is in session, the recess appointee may not be paid from the Treasury until he or she is confirmed by the Senate. The salary prohibition does not apply (1) if the vacancy arose within 30 days before the end of the session; (2) if a nomination for the office (other than the nomination of someone given a recess appointment during the preceding recess) was pending when the Senate recessed; or (3) if a nomination was rejected within 30 days before the end of the session and another individual was given the recess appointment. A recess appointment falling under any one of these three exceptions must be followed by a nomination to the position not later than 40 days after the beginning of the next session of the Senate. For this reason, when a recess appointment is made, the President generally submits a new nomination for the appointee even when an earlier nomination is still pending.[15] In addition, although a recess appointee whose nomination to a full term is subsequently rejected by the Senate may continue to serve until the end of his or her recess appointment, a provision of the FY2008 Financial Services and General Government Appropriations Act might prevent an appointee from being paid after his or her rejection.[16]

During the 110th Congress, the Senate employed, apparently for the first time, another method intended to restrict the President's recess appointment power. This method is predicated on the notion that the President could be restricted from making a recess appointment during a period of three days or less. The Constitution does not specify the length of time that the Senate must be in recess before the President may make a recess appointment. Over the last century, as shorter recesses have become more commonplace, the Department of Justice has offered differing views on this issue. In 1993, however, a Justice Department brief implied that the President may make a recess appointment during a recess of more than three days. The authors reasoned that because the "Constitution restricts the Senate's ability to adjourn its session for more than three days without obtaining the consent of the House ... [i]t might be argued that this means that the Framers did not consider one, two and three day recesses to be constitutionally significant."[17] As a practical matter, the shortest recess during which appointments have been made during the past 20 years was 10 days.

From November 2007 through the end of the Bush presidency, the Senate structured its recesses in a way that was intended, at least initially, to prevent the President from making recess appointments by preventing the occurrence of a recess of more than three days.[18] On November 16, 2007, the Senate majority leader announced that the Senate would "be coming in for pro forma sessions during the Thanksgiving holiday to prevent recess appointments."[19] The Senate recessed later that day, and pro forma meetings[20] were convened on November 20, 23, 27, and 29, with no business conducted. The Senate next conducted business after reconvening on December 3, 2007. Similar procedures were followed during other periods, during the remainder of President Bush's term, that would otherwise have been Senate recesses of a week or longer in duration.[21] The President made no recess appointments between the initial pro forma sessions in November 2007 and the end of his presidency.

Characterization of Regulatory and Other Collegial Bodies

Federal executive branch boards and commissions discussed in this report share, among other characteristics, the following: (1) they are independent executive branch bodies located, with four exceptions, outside executive departments;[22] (2) several members head each entity; (3) the members are appointed by the President with the advice and consent of the Senate; and (4) the members serve fixed terms of office, and, except in a few bodies, the President's power to remove them is restricted.

For most of the boards included in this report, the fixed terms of office for the member positions have set beginning and end dates, irrespective of whether the posts are filled or when appointments are made.[23] The end dates of the fixed terms of a board's members are staggered, so that the terms do not expire all at once. The use of terms with fixed beginning and end dates is intended to minimize the occurrence of simultaneous board member departures and thereby increase leadership continuity.

Under such an arrangement, an individual is nominated to a particular position and a particular term of office. An individual may be nominated and confirmed for a position for the remainder of an unexpired term in order to replace an appointee who has resigned (or died). Alternatively, an individual might be nominated for an upcoming term with the expectation that the new term will be underway by the time of confirmation. Occasionally, where the unexpired term has been for a very short period, the President has submitted two nominations of the same person simultaneously—the first to complete the unexpired term and the second to complete the entire succeeding term of office.

On some commissions, the chair is subject to Senate confirmation and must be appointed from among the incumbent commissioners. If the President wishes to appoint, as chair, someone who is not on the commission, two nominations are submitted simultaneously for the nominee—one for member and the other for chair.

As independent entities with staggered membership, executive branch boards and commissions have more political independence from the President than do executive departments. Nonetheless, the President can sometimes exercise significant influence over the composition of the membership when he designates the chair or has the opportunity to fill a number of vacancies at once. For example, President George W. Bush had the opportunity to shape the Securities and Exchange Commission during the first two years of his presidency because of existing vacancies, resignations, and the death of a member. Likewise, during the same time period, President Bush was able to submit nominations for all of the positions on the National Labor Relations Board because of existing vacancies, expiring recess appointments, and resignations. Simultaneous turnover of board or commission membership may result from coincidence, but it may also be the result of a buildup of vacancies after extended periods during which the President fails to nominate, or the Senate fails to confirm, members.

Two other notable characteristics apply to appointments to some of the boards and commissions. First, for 26 of the boards and commissions in this report, the law limits the number of appointed members who may belong to the same political party, usually to no more than a simple majority of the appointed members (e.g., two of three, or three of five).[24] Second, advice and consent requirements also apply to inspector general appointments in four of these organizations and general counsel appointments in three.

Appointments During the 110th Congress

During the 110th Congress, President George W. Bush submitted nominations to the Senate for 74 of the 152 full-time positions on 34 regulatory and other boards and commissions. (Most of the remaining positions were not vacant during that time.) A total of 88 nominations were submitted for these positions, of which 46 were confirmed, 15 were withdrawn, and 27 were returned to the President. The number of nominations exceeded the number of positions because the President submitted multiple nominations for some positions. In some cases, for example, the President submitted one nomination for the end of a term in progress and a second nomination of the same person to the same position for the succeeding term. In other cases, the President submitted a second nomination after his first choice failed to be confirmed. The President also submitted an "extra" nomination of the one individual to whom he had given a recess appointment in order to comply with a law affecting the payment of that appointee (see "Recess Appointments," above). **Table 1** summarizes the appointment activity for the 110th Congress. At the end of the Congress, 15 incumbents were serving past the expiration of their terms.[25] In addition, there were 22 vacancies among the 152 positions.

Length of Time to Confirm a Nomination

The length of time a given nomination may be pending in the Senate has varied widely. Some nominations have been confirmed within a few days; others have been confirmed within several months; and some have never been confirmed. In the board and commission profiles following this opening narrative, this report provides, for each board or commission nomination that was confirmed in the 110th Congress, the number of days between nomination and confirmation ("days to confirm"). For those nominations that were confirmed, an average of 148 days elapsed between nomination and confirmation. The median[26] number of days elapsed was 90. The difference between these two numbers suggests that the average was pulled upward by a small number of unusually high numbers.

A Change in Methodology From Previous Tracking Reports

The calculations of nomination-to-confirmation intervals provided in this report counted all the days within such intervals, including those during summer recesses and between sessions of the Senate. The inclusion of all days differs from the methodology used in similar CRS reports for previous Congresses.[27] In these earlier reports, days during August and intersession recesses were not included in calculations of nomination-to-confirmation intervals. These changes may reduce the comparability of statistics provided in this report with those provided in earlier reports. More information on this change in methodology is available in **Appendix D.**

Table 1. Appointment Action for Regulatory and Other Collegial Boards and Commissions. 110th Congress, 2007-2008.

Positions on boards and commissions (total)	152
Positions to which nominations were made	74
Individual nominees	79
Nominations submitted to the Senate during the 110th Congress (total)	88
Disposition of nominations	
Confirmed by the Senate	46
Withdrawn	15
Returned	27
Recess Appointments (total)	1

Source: The information in this table summarizes data presented in Table A-2.

Organization of the Report

Board and Commission Profiles

Each of the 34 board or commission profiles following the narrative portion of this report is organized into three parts: a paragraph discussing the body's organizational structure, a table identifying its membership as of the end of the 110th Congress, and a table listing nominations and appointments to its positions during the 110th Congress. The organizational sections discuss the statutory requirements for the appointed positions, including the number of members on each board or commission, their terms of office, whether or not they may continue in their positions after their terms expire, whether or not political balance is required, and the method for selection of the chair.

Data[28] on appointment actions during the 110th Congress appear under both the sections entitled "Membership as of the End of the 110th Congress" and those entitled "Appointment Action in the 110th Congress." The former identify the agencies' positions requiring Senate confirmation and the incumbents in those positions as of that time. Incumbents whose terms have expired are italicized. Most of the incumbents serve fixed terms of office and are removable only for specified causes. They generally remain in office when a new administration assumes office following a presidential election. For those agencies requiring political balance among their members, the party affiliation of an incumbent is listed as Democrat (D), Republican (R), or

Independent (I). The section also includes the pay levels of the positions. For presidentially appointed positions requiring Senate confirmation, the pay levels fall under the Executive Schedule, which ranges from level I, for cabinet-level offices, to level V, for the lowest-ranked positions. Most of the chair positions are at level III, and most of the other positions are at level IV.[29]

The "Appointment Action" section provides information about each nomination, in chronological order, including the name of the nominee, the position to which he or she was nominated, the date of submission, the date of confirmation (if any), and the number of days that elapsed between submission and confirmation. Actions other than confirmation (i.e., nominations rejected by the Senate, nominations returned to or withdrawn by the President, and recess appointments) are also noted. Occasionally, where a position was vacant and the unexpired term of office was to end within a number of weeks or months, two nominations for the same nominee were submitted: the first to complete the unexpired term, and the second for a full term following completion of the expired term. Also, in the single instance during the 110th Congress where the President gave a recess appointment to a nominee for a position covered by this report while the nomination was awaiting Senate action, a second, follow-up nomination was submitted to comply with the requirements of 5 U.S.C. § 5503(b).

In tables that show more than one confirmed nomination, the mean number of days to confirm a nomination is provided. This figure was determined by calculating the number of days between the nomination and confirmation dates, adding these numbers for all confirmed nominations, and dividing the result by the number of nominations confirmed. For tables in which one individual was confirmed more than once (to be a chair and a member, for example), the mean was calculated by averaging all values in the "Days to confirm" column, including the values for both confirmations.

Additional Appointment Information

Appendix A provides two tables. **Table A-1** includes information on each of the nominations and appointments to regulatory and other collegial boards and commissions during the 110th Congress, alphabetically organized, and following a similar format to that of the "Appointment Action" sections just discussed. It identifies the board or commission involved and the dates of nomination and confirmation. The appendix also indicates if a nomination was withdrawn, returned, or rejected, or if a recess appointment was made. The mean and median number of days taken to confirm a nomination are also provided.[30]

Table A-2 provides summary information on appointments and nominations by organization. For each of the 34 independent boards and commissions discussed in this report, the appendix provides the number of positions, vacancies, incumbents whose term has expired, nominations, individual nominees, positions to which nominations were made, confirmations, nominations returned to the President, nominations withdrawn, and recess appointments.

Appendix B provides information concerning Senate recesses during the 110th Congress. A list of organization abbreviations can be found in **Appendix C**.

As noted above, this report employs certain methods that differ from those of previous similar reports. These methodological changes are discussed in detail in **Appendix D**.

CHEMICAL SAFETY AND HAZARD INVESTIGATION BOARD (CSB)

The CSB is an independent agency consisting of five members (no political balance is required), including a chair, who serve five-year terms. The President appoints the members, including the chair, with the advice and consent of the Senate. When a term expires, the incumbent must leave office. (42 U.S.C. § 7412(r)(6))

CSB Membership as of the End of the 110th Congress.

Incumbent	Party [a]	Date first confirmed	Term expires	Pay level
John S. Bresland (Chair)	na	08/01/02	03/14/13	IV
Gary L. Visscher	na	11/21/04	11/29/09	IV
William B. Wark	na	09/15/06	09/22/11	IV
William E. Wright	na	09/15/06	09/22/11	IV
Vacant			[b]	IV

a The abbreviation "na" means not applicable.

b The term of an appointment to this vacant position would expire five years from the appointment date.

CSB Appointment Action During the 110th Congress.

Nominee/ Recess appointee	Party[a]	Position	To replace	Date nominated	Date confirmed	Days to confirm
John S. Bresland	na	Member	Reappointment	07/11/07	03/13/08	246
John S. Bresland	na	Chair	Carolyn W. Merritt	07/11/07	03/13/08	246
Charles R. H. Shearer	na	Member	Carolyn W. Merritt	07/11/07	Returned 01/02/09[b]	

a The abbreviation "na" means not applicable.

b Returned to the President at the end of the 110th Congress under the provisions of Senate Rule XXXI, paragraph 6 of the Standing Rules of the Senate.

COMMODITY FUTURES TRADING COMMISSION (CFTC)

The CFTC consists of five members (no more than three may be from the same political party) who serve five-year terms. At the end of a term, a member may remain in office, unless replaced, until the end of the next session of Congress. The chair is also appointed by the President, with the advice and consent of the Senate. (7 U.S.C. § 2(a)(2))

CFTC Membership as of the End of the 110th Congress.

Incumbent	Party	confirmed	Term expires	level
Walter Lukken (Acting Chair)	R	08/01/02	04/13/10	III
Michael V. Dunn	D	11/21/04	06/19/11	IV
Jill E. Sommers	R	08/01/07	04/13/09	IV
Bartholomew H. Chilton[a]	D	08/01/07	04/13/08	IV
Vacant			04/13/12	IV

a. The term of the incumbent shown in italics had expired. He continued to serve under the holdover provision noted above.

CFTC Appointment Action During the 110th Congress.

Nominee/Recess appointee	Party	Position	To replace	Date nominated	Date confirmed	Days to confirm
Jill E. Sommers	R	Commissioner	Sharon Brown-Hruska	05/03/07	08/01/07	90
Bartholomew H. Chilton	D	Commissioner	Frederick W. Hatfield	05/03/07	08/01/07	90
Walter Lukken	R	Chair	Reuben Jeffrey III	08/07/07	Returned 01/02/09[a]	
Bartholomew H. Chilton	D	Commissioner	Reappointment	04/03/08	Returned 01/02/09[a]	
Scott O'Malia	[b]	Commissioner	Reuben Jeffrey III	04/03/08	Returned 01/02/09[a]	

a Returned to the President at the end of the 110th Congress under the provisions of Senate Rule XXXI, paragraph 6 of the Standing Rules of the Senate.

b Party affiliation is unknown.

Consumer Product Safety Commission (CPSC)

The statute establishing the CPSC calls for five members, who serve seven-year terms. During a period that included the 110th Congress, however, funding was authorized for only three of these positions. No more than three of the members may be from the same political party. A member may remain in office for one year at the end of a term, unless replaced. The chair is also appointed by the President, with the advice and consent of the Senate. (15 U.S.C. § 2053)

CPSC Membership as of the End of the 110th Congress.

Incumbent	Party	Date first confirmed	Term expires	Pay level
Nancy A. Nord (Acting Chair)	R	04/28/05	10/26/12	III[a]
Thomas H. Moore	D	04/06/95	10/26/10	IV
Vacant			10/26/13	IV
Vacant			10/26/11	IV
Vacant			10/26/14	IV

Note: From FY1993 through the period covered by this report, funds were not available for the compensation and benefits of more than three members of the commission. (P.L. 102-389, Title 3, October 6, 1992; 105 Stat. 1596) P.L. 110-314, § 202(b) (122 Stat. 3040) repealed this provision, effective August 14, 2009.

a. According to an agency official, Commissioner Nord was to be paid at level IV while she was acting chair.

CPSC Appointment Action During the 110th Congress.

Nominee/ Recess appointee	Party	Position	To replace	Date nominated	Date confirmed	Days to confirm
Michael E. Baroody	R	Commissioner	Harold D. Stratton	03/05/07	Withdrawn 05/23/07	
Michael E. Baroody	R	Chair	Harold D. Stratton	03/05/07	Withdrawn 05/23/07	

Defense Nuclear Facilities Safety Board (DNFSB)

The DNFSB consists of five members (no more than three may be from the same political party), who serve five-year terms. After a term expires, a member may continue to serve until a successor takes office. The President designates the chair and vice chair. (42 U.S.C. § 2286)

DNFSB Membership as of the End of the 110th Congress.

Incumbent	Party	Date first confirmed	Term expires	Pay level
Andrew J. Eggenberger[a] (Chair)	R	10/18/89	10/18/08	III
John E. Mansfield (Vice Chair)	R	10/30/97	10/18/11	III
Joseph F. Bader[a]	D	11/21/04	10/18/07	III
Larry W. Brown	R	09/29/06	10/18/10	III
Peter S. Winokur	D	09/29/06	10/18/09	III

a The terms of the incumbents shown in italics had expired. They continued to serve under the holdover provision noted above.

DNFSB Appointment Action During the 110th Congress.

Nominee/Recess appointee	Party	Position	To replace	Date nominated	Date confirmed	Days to confirm
Joseph F. Bader	D	Member	Reappointment	06/26/08	Returned 01/02/09[a]	
Ambrose L. Schwallie	[b]	Member	Andrew J. Eggenberger	07/23/08	Returned 01/02/09[a]	

a Returned to the President at the end of the 110th Congress under the provisions of Senate Rule XXXI, paragraph 6 of the Standing Rules of the Senate.
b Party affiliation is unknown.

ELECTION ASSISTANCE COMMISSION (EAC)

The EAC consists of four members (no more than two may be from the same political party), who serve four-year terms. After a term expires, a member may continue to serve until a successor takes office. The chair and vice chair, from different political parties and designated by the commission, change each year. (42 U.S.C. § 15323)

EAC Membership as of the End of the 110th Congress.

Incumbent	Party	Date first confirmed	Term expires	Pay level
Rosemary E. Rodriguez (Chair)	D	02/15/07	12/12/11	IV
Donetta Davidson (Vice Chair)	R	07/28/05	12/12/11	IV
Gracia M. Hillman	D	12/09/03	12/12/09	IV
Gineen B. Beach	a	10/02/08	12/12/09	IV

a. Party affiliation is unknown.

EAC Appointment Action During the 110th Congress.

Nominee/Recess appointee	Party	Position	To replace	Date nominated	Date confirmed	Days to confirm
Rosemary E. Rodriguez	D	Member	Raymundo Martinez III	01/09/07	02/15/07	37
Caroline C. Hunter	R	Member	Paul S. DeGregorio	01/09/07	02/15/07	37
Gracia M. Hillman	D	Member	Reappointment	06/13/07	10/02/08	477
Donetta Davidson	R	Member	Reappointment	05/08/08	10/02/08	147
Rosemary E. Rodriguez	D	Member	Reappointment	05/08/08	10/02/08	147
Gineen B. Beach	a	Member	Caroline C. Hunter	07/31/08	10/02/08	63
Mean number of days to confirm a nomination						151

a. Party affiliation is unknown.

Equal Employment Opportunity Commission (EEOC)

The EEOC consists of five members (no more than three may be from the same political party), who serve five-year terms. An incumbent whose term has expired may continue to serve until a successor is appointed, except that no such member may continue to serve (1) for more than 60 days when Congress is in session, unless a successor has been nominated; or (2) after the adjournment of the session of the Senate in which the successor's nomination was submitted. The President designates the chair and the vice chair. The

President also appoints the general counsel, with the advice and consent of the Senate. (42 U.S.C. § 2000e-4)

EEOC Membership as of the End of the 110th Congress.

Incumbent	Party	Date first confirmed	Term expires	Pay level
Commissioners				
Naomi C. Earp (Chair)	R	10/31/03	07/01/10	III
Stuart Ishimaru	D	10/31/03	07/01/12	IV
Christine M. Griffin	D	10/21/05	07/01/09	IV
Constance S. Barker	R	03/27/08	07/01/11	IV
Vacant			07/01/13	IV
General Counsel[a]				
Ronald S. Cooper	na	03/27/06	4 years from appointment	V

a. The abbreviation "na" means not applicable. The provision establishing the general counsel position does not include requirements with regard to political affiliation.

EEOC Appointment Action During the 110th Congress.

Nominee/Recess appointee	Party	Position	To replace	Date nominated	Date confirmed	Days to confirm
David Palmer	R	Member	Cari M. Dominguez	01/09/07	Withdrawn 09/04/07	
Stuart Ishimaru	D	Member	Reappointment	08/03/07	12/19/07 138	
Constance S. Barker	R	Member	Cari M. Dominguez	03/31/08	06/27/08 88	
Mean number of days to confirm a nomination				113		

EXPORT-IMPORT BANK BOARD OF DIRECTORS (EXIMBANK)

The Export-Import Bank Board of Directors comprises the bank president, who serves as chair; the bank first vice president, who serves as vice chair; and three other members (no more than three of these five may be from the same political party). All five members are appointed by the President, with the advice and consent of the Senate, and serve four-year terms. An incumbent whose term has expired may continue to serve until a successor is qualified, or until six months after the term expires—whichever occurs earlier. (12 U.S.C. § 635a) The President also appoints an inspector general, with the advice and consent of the Senate. (5 U.S.C. App., Inspector General Act of 1978, § 3, 12)

EXIMBANK Membership as of the End of the 110th Congress.

Incumbent	Party	Date first confirmed	Term expires	Pay level
Board of Directors				
James H. Lambright (President/Chair)	R	07/26/06	01/20/09	III
Linda M. Conlin (Vice President/Vice Chair)	R	11/21/04	01/20/09	IV
J. Joseph Grandmaison	D	12/20/01	01/20/09	IV
Bijan Rafiekian[a]	R	09/29/06	01/20/11	IV
Diane G. Farrell	[b]	05/24/07	01/20/11	IV
Inspector General				
Michael W. Tankersley	na	06/28/07	indefinite	[c]

a Rafiekian was known as Bijan R. Kian on the EXIMBANK Website http://www.exim.gov.

b Party affiliation is unknown.

c The abbreviation "na" means not applicable. The provision establishing the inspector general position does not include requirements with regard to political affiliation. This position does not have a fixed term. As of the end of the 110th Congress, the Inspector General Act provided as follows: "An Inspector General may be removed from office by the President. If an Inspector General is removed from office or is transferred to another position or location within an establishment, the President shall communicate in writing the reasons for any such removal or transfer to both Houses of Congress, not later than 30 days before the removal or transfer. Nothing in [this provision] shall prohibit a personnel action otherwise authorized by law, other than transfer or removal." (5 U.S.C. App., § 3(b)). "The annual rate of basic pay for an Inspector General ... shall be the rate payable for level III of the Executive Schedule ... plus 3 percent." (5 U.S.C. App., § 3 (e))

EXIMBANK Appointment Action During the 110th Congress.

Nominee/Recess appointee	Party	Position	To replace	Date nominated	Date confirmed	Days to confirm
Michael W. Tankersley	na[a]	Inspector General	New position	01/09/07	06/28/07	170
Bijan Rafiekian	R	Member	Reappointment	02/16/07	08/01/07	166
Diane G. Farrell	[b]	Member	J. Max Cleland	05/24/07	08/01/07	69
Mean number of days to confirm a nomination				135		

a The abbreviation "na" means not applicable.
b Party affiliation is unknown.

FARM CREDIT ADMINISTRATION (FCA)

The FCA consists of three members (no more than two may be from the same political party), who serve six-year terms. A member may not succeed himself or herself unless he or she was first appointed to complete an unexpired term of three years or less. A member whose term expires may continue to serve until a successor takes office. The President designates the chair. (12 U.S.C. § 2242)

FCA Membership as of the End of the 110th Congress.

Incumbent	Party	Date first confirmed	Term expires	Pay level
Leland A. Strom (Chair)	R	12/09/06	10/13/12	III
Nancy C. Pellett[a]	R	11/14/02	05/21/08	IV
Dallas Tonsager	D	11/21/04	05/21/10	IV

a. The term of the incumbent shown in italics had expired. She continued to serve under the holdover provision noted above.

FCA Appointment Action During the 110th Congress.

Nominee/Recess appointee	Party	Position	To replace	Date nominated	Date confirmed	Days to confirm
Mark E. Keenum	R	Member	Nancy C. Pellett	06/26/08	Returned 01/02/09[a]	

a. Returned to the President at the end of the 110th Congress under the provisions of Senate Rule XXXI, paragraph 6 of the Standing Rules of the Senate.

FEDERAL COMMUNICATIONS COMMISSION (FCC)

The FCC consists of five members (no more than three may be from the same political party), who serve five-year terms. When a term expires, a member may continue to serve until the end of the next session of Congress, unless a successor is appointed before that time. The President designates the chair. (47 U.S.C. § 154)

FCC Membership as of the End of the 110th Congress.

Incumbent	Party	Date first confirmed	Term expires	Pay level
Kevin J. Martin (Chair)	R	05/25/01	06/30/11	III
Michael J. Copps	D	05/25/01	06/30/10	IV
Jonathan S. Adelsteina	D	11/14/02	06/30/08	IV
Deborah T. Tate[a]	R	12/21/05	06/30/07	IV
Robert M. McDowell	R	05/26/06	06/30/09	IV

a. The term of the incumbents shown in italics had expired. They continued to serve under the holdover provision noted above.

FCC Appointment Action During the 110th Congress.

Nominee/Recess appointee	Party	Position	To replace	Date nominated	Date confirmed	Days to confirm
Deborah T. Tate	R	Member	Reappointment	06/21/07	Returned 01/02/09[a]	
Jonathan S. Adelstein	D	Member	Reappointment	12/03/07	Returned 01/02/09[a]	

a. Returned to the President at the end of the 110th Congress under the provisions of Senate Rule XXXI, paragraph 6 of the Standing Rules of the Senate.

Federal Deposit Insurance Corporation Board of Directors (FDIC)

The FDIC board of directors consists of five members, of whom two—the comptroller of the currency and the director of the Office of Thrift Supervision (OTS)—are *ex officio*. The three appointed members serve six-year terms. An appointed member may continue to serve after the expiration of a term until a successor is appointed. Not more than three of the members of the board of directors may be from the same political party. The President appoints the chair and the vice chair, with the advice and consent of the Senate, from among the appointed members. The chair is appointed for a term of five years. (12 U.S.C.§ 1812) The President also appoints the inspector general, with the advice and consent of the Senate. (5 U.S.C. App., Inspector General Act of 1978, § 3, 12)

Full-Time FDIC Membership as of the End of the 110th Congress.

Incumbent	Party	Date first confirmed	Term expires	Pay level
Board of Directors				
Sheila C. Bair (Chair)	R	06/15/06	07/15/13	III
Martin J. Gruenberg (Vice Chair)	D	07/29/05	12/27/12	IV
Thomas J. Curry	I	12/09/03	12/12/09	IV
Inspector General				
Jon T. Rymer	na	06/22/06	Indefinite	a

a. The abbreviation "na" means not applicable. The provision establishing the inspector general position does not include requirements with regard to political affiliation. This position does not have a fixed term. As of the end of the 110th Congress, the Inspector General Act provided as follows: "An Inspector General may be removed from office by the President. If an Inspector General is removed from office or is transferred to another position or location within an establishment, the President shall communicate in writing the reasons for any such removal or transfer to both Houses of Congress, not later than 30 days before the removal or transfer. Nothing in [this provision] shall prohibit a personnel action otherwise authorized by law, other than transfer or removal." (5 U.S.C. App., § 3(b)) "The annual rate of basic pay for an Inspector General ... shall be the rate payable for level III of the Executive Schedule ... plus 3 percent." (5 U.S.C. App., § 3(e))

No FDIC Appointment Action to Full-Time Positions During the 110th Congress

FEDERAL ELECTION COMMISSION (FEC)

The FEC consists of six members (no more than three may be from the same political party), who may serve for a single term of six-years. When a term expires, a member may continue to serve until a successor takes office. The chair and vice chair, from different political parties and elected by the commission, change each year. Generally, the vice chair succeeds the chair. (2 U.S.C. § 437c)

FEC Membership as of the End of the 110th Congress.

Incumbent	Party	Date first confirmed	Term expires	Pay level
Donald F. McGahn II (Chair)	R	06/24/08	04/30/09	IV
Steven T. Walther (Vice Chair)	I	01/09/07	04/30/09	IV
Ellen L. Weintraub[a]	D	03/18/03	04/30/07	IV
Cynthia L. Bauerly	D	06/24/08	04/30/11	IV
Caroline C. Hunter	R	06/24/08	04/30/13	IV
Matthew S. Petersen	R	06/24/08	04/30/11	IV

a. The term of the incumbent shown in italics had expired. She continued to serve under the holdover provision noted above.

FEC Appointment Action During the 110th Congress.

Nominee/recess appointee	Party	Position	To replace	Date nominated	Date confirmed	Days to confirm
Steven T. Walther	I	Member	Scott E. Thomas	01/09/07	06/24/08	532
Hans von Spakovsky	R	Member	Bradley A. Smith	01/09/07	Withdrawn 05/20/08	
David M. Mason	R	Member	Reappointmenta	01/09/07	Withdrawn 05/06/08	
Robert D. Lenhard	D	Member	Danny L. McDonald	01/09/07	Withdrawn 05/06/08	
Cynthia L. Bauerly	D	Member	Robert D. Lenhard	05/06/08	06/24/08	49

FEC Appointment Action During the 110th Congress (Continued).

Nominee/recess appointee	Party	Position	To replace	Date nominated	Date confirm	Days to
Caroline C. Hunter	R	Member	Michael E. Toner	05/06/08	06/24/08	49
Donald F. McGahn II	R	Member	David M. Mason	05/06/08	06/24/08	49
Matthew S. Petersen	R	Member	Hans von Spakovsky	06/12/08	06/24/08	12
Mean number of days to confirm a nomination					138	

a. Since 1998, new FEC members have been authorized to serve for only one term. Mason was first selected for office before that time, and would therefore have been eligible for reappointment.

Federal Energy Regulatory Commission (FERC)

The FERC, an independent agency within the Department of Energy, consists of five members (no more than three may be from the same political party), who serve five-year terms. When a term expires, a member may continue to serve until a successor takes office, except that such commissioner may not serve beyond the end of the session of the Congress in which his or her term expires. The President designates the chair. (42 U.S.C. § 7171)

FERC Membership as of the End of the 110th Congress.

Incumbent	Party	Date first confirmed	Term expires	Pay level
Joseph T. Kelliher (Chair)	R	11/07/03	06/30/12	III
Suedeen G. Kelly	D	11/07/03	06/30/09	IV
Jon Wellinghoff	D	07/14/06	06/30/13	IV
Philip D. Moeller	R	07/14/06	06/30/10	IV
Marc Spitzer	R	07/14/06	06/30/11	IV

FERC Appointment Action During the 110th Congress.

Nominee/ Recess appointee	Party	Position	To replace	Date nominated	Date confirmed	Days to confirm
Joseph T. Kelliher	R	Commissioner	Reappointment	03/07/07	12/19/07	287
Jon Wellinghoff	D	Commissioner	Reappointment	12/11/07	12/19/07	8
Mean number of days to confirm a nomination				148		

FEDERAL HOUSING FINANCE BOARD (FHFB)

The FHFB consisted of five members, of whom one—the Secretary of Housing and Urban Development (HUD) or his or her designee—was *ex officio*. The Housing and Economic Recovery Act of 2008 (P.L. 110-289; 122 Stat. 2654) provided for the abolishment of this board, effective one year from the statute's July 30, 2008, enactment (§ 1311; 122 Stat. 2797). Prior to the enactment of this statute, the law provided for four appointed members who served seven-year terms, with no more than three from the same political party. An appointed member whose term expiresdcould continue to serve until a successor was appointed. The President designated the chair from among the appointed members. (12 U.S.C. § 1422a(1)) Section 1204 of the act (122 Stat. 2785) repealed this section, but it was in effect during part of the period covered by this report.

Full-Time FHFB Membership as of the End of the 110th Congress.

Incumbent	Party	Date first confirmed	Term expires	Pay level
Ronald A. Rosenfeld (Chair)	R	03/16/05	02/27/09	III
Allan I. Mendelowitz	D	11/29/01	02/27/14	IV
Alicia K. Castaneda	R	12/09/03	02/27/11	IV
Geoffrey S. Bacino	D	07/26/06	02/27/13	IV

FHFB Appointment Action to Full-Time Positions During the 110th Congress.

Nominee/Recess appointee	Party	Position	To replace	Date nominated	Date confirmed	Days to confirm
Allan I. Mendelowitz	D	Director	Reappointment	10/18/07	12/19/07	62

FEDERAL LABOR RELATIONS AUTHORITY (FLRA)

The FLRA consists of three members (no more than two may be from the same political party), who serve five-year terms. After the date on which a five-year term would expire, a member may continue to serve until the end of the next Congress, unless a successor is appointed before that time. The President designates the chair. The general counsel is also appointed by the President, with the advice and consent of the Senate. (5 U.S.C. § 7104)

FLRA Membership as of the End of the 110th Congress.

Incumbent	Party	Date first confirmed	Term expires	Pay level
Members				
Thomas M. Beck (Chair)	R	10/02/08	07/01/10	IV
Carol W. Pope	D	10/26/00	07/01/09	V
Vacant			07/29/12	V
General Counsel[a]				
Vacant	na	Five years		V

a. The abbreviation "na" means not applicable. The provision establishing the general counsel position does not include requirements with regard to political affiliation. The general counsel is appointed for a five-year term.

FLRA Appointment Action During the 110th Congress.

Nominee/Recess appointee	Party	Position	To replace	Date nominated	Date confirmed	Days to confirm
Wayne C. Beyer	R	Member	Othoniel Armendariz	01/09/07	Withdrawn 12/14/07	
Dale Cabaniss	R	Member	Reappointment	03/12/07	Withdrawn 06/28/07	
Carol W. Pope	D	Member	Reappointment	03/12/07	Returned 01/02/09[a]	
Carol W. Pope	D	Member	Recess Appointment 04/04/07[b]			
Carol W. Pope	D	Member	Reappointment	05/16/07	10/02/08[c]	505
Thomas M. Beck	R	Member	Dale Cabaniss	06/28/07	Withdrawn 12/14/07	
Thomas M. Beck	R	Member	Wayne C. Beyer	12/14/07	10/02/08	293
Brandon C. Bungard	R	General	Colleen D. Kiko	04/02/08	Returned 01/02/09[a]	
Mean number of days to confirm		Counsel			399	

a Returned to the President at the end of the 110th Congress under the provisions of Senate Rule XXXI, paragraph 6 of the Standing Rules of the Senate.

b Pope was recess appointed to a seat with a term that was to expire July 1, 2009. Recess appointments are always limited in duration, however, regardless of the term of office of a particular position. In this case, Pope's recess appointment would have expired at the end of second session of the 110th Congress by which time she had been confirmed.

c When a recess appointment is made, the President generally submits a new nomination for the nominee, even when an old nomination is pending, in compliance with 5 U.S.C. § 5503. In this case one nomination was returned and one nomination was confirmed.

Federal Maritime Commission (FMC)

The FMC consists of five members (no more than three may be from the same political party), who serve five-year terms. When a term expires, a member may continue to serve until a successor takes office. The President designates the chair. (46 U.S.C. § 301)

FMC Membership as of the End of the 110th Congress.

Incumbent	Party	Date first confirmed	Term expires	Pay level
Joseph E. Brennan[a]	D	11/10/99	06/30/08	IV
Harold J. Creel, Jr.	D	08/17/94	06/30/09	IV
Rebecca F. Dye	R	11/14/02	06/30/10	IV
Vacant			06/30/12	IV
Vacant			06/30/11	IV

Note: As of the end of the 110th Congress, the FMC had no presidentially designated chair. At that time, the most recent chair was Steven R. Blust, who had left the agency on June 30, 2006. A presidentially designated chair would be compensated at Level III of the Executive Schedule.

a. The term of the incumbent shown in italics has expired. He continued to serve under the holdover provision noted above.

FMC Appointment Action During the 110th Congress.

Nominee/Recess appointee	Party	Position	To replace	Date nominated	Date confirmed	Days to confirm
Carl B. Kress	R	Commissioner	Steven R. Blust	08/02/07	Returned 01/02/09a	
A. Paul Anderson	R	Commissioner	Reappointment	08/02/07	Withdrawn 05/20/08	
Sean T. Connaughton	R	Commissioner	A. Paul Anderson	09/09/08	Returned 01/02/09a	

a. Returned to the President at the end of the 110th Congress under the provisions of Senate Rule XXXI, paragraph 6 of the Standing Rules of the Senate.

Federal Mine Safety and Health Review Commission (FMSHRC)

The FMSHRC consists of five members (no political balance is required), who serve six-year terms. When a term expires, the member must leave office. The President designates the chair. (30 U.S.C. § 823)

FMSHRC Membership as of the End of the 110th Congress.

Incumbent	Party[a]	Date first confirmed	Term expires	Pay level
Michael F. Duffy (Chair)	na	11/19/02	08/30/12	III
Mary L. Jordan	na	04/14/94	08/30/14	IV
Michael G. Young	na	07/31/03	08/30/14	IV
Robert F. Cohen Jr.	na	03/13/08	08/30/12	IV
Vacant	na		08/30/10	IV

a. The abbreviation "na" means not applicable.

FMSHRC Appointment Action During the 110th Congress.

Nominee/ Recess appointee	Party [a]	Position	To replace	Date nominated	Date confirmed	Days to confirm
Arlene Holen	na	Commission er	Robert H. Beatty Jr.	01/09/07	Withdrawn 05/20/08	
Michael F. Duffy	na	Commission er	Reappointment	01/09/07	03/13/08 429	
Robert F. Cohen Jr.	na	Commission er	Stanley C. Suboleski	12/12/07	03/13/08 92	
Mary L. Jordan	na	Commission er	Reappointment	06/26/08	10/02/08 98	
Michael G. Young	na	Commission er	Reappointment	09/08/08	10/02/08 24	
Mean number of days to confirm a nomination				161		

a. The abbreviation "na" means not applicable.

Federal Reserve System Board of Governors (FRS)

The FRS consists of seven members (no political balance is required), who serve 14-year terms. When a term expires, a member may continue to serve until a successor takes office. The President appoints the chair and vice chair, who are separately appointed as members, for four-year terms, with the advice and consent of the Senate. (12 U.S.C. §§ 241, 242)

FRS Membership as of the End of the 110th Congress.

Incumbent	Party[a]	Date first confirmed	Term expires	Pay level
Ben S. Bernanke (Chair)	na	07/31/02[b]	01/31/20[c]	I
Donald L. Kohn (Vice Chair)	na	07/31/02	01/31/16[c]	II
Randall S. Kroszner[d]	na	02/17/06	01/31/08	II
Kevin M. Warsh	na	02/17/06	01/31/18	II
Elizabeth A. Duke	na	06/27/08	01/31/12	II
Vacant	na		01/31/14	II
Vacant	na		01/31/10	II

a The abbreviation "na" means not applicable.

b Bernanke was initially confirmed July 31, 2002, to the unexpired term of Edward W. Kelly. That term would have expired January 31, 2004. He was then reappointed for a term that would have expired January 31, 2018, but he resigned to become a member of the Council of Economic Advisors. On November 1, 2005, Bernanke was nominated to succeed Alan Greenspan as a member and as chair. He was confirmed to both positions on January 31, 2006.

c Bernanke's term as a member expires on January 31, 2020. His term as chair expired on January 31, 2010. Kohn's term as a member expires on January 31, 2016. His term as vice chair expired on June 23, 2010.

d The term of the incumbent shown in italics had expired. He continued to serve under the holdover provision noted above.

FRS Appointment Action During the 110th Congress.

Nominee/ Recess appointee	Party[a]	Position	To replace	Date nominated	Date confirmed	Days to confirm
Elizabeth A. Duke	na	Member	Susan S. Bies	05/16/07	06/27/08	408
Larry A. Klane	na	Member	Mark W. Olson	05/16/07	Returned 01/02/09[b]	
Randall S. Kroszner	na	Member	Reappointment	05/16/07	Returned 01/02/09[b]	

a The abbreviation "na" means not applicable.

b Returned to the President at the end of the 110th Congress under the provisions of Senate Rule XXXI, paragraph 6 of the Standing Rules of the Senate.

FEDERAL TRADE COMMISSION (FTC)

The FTC consists of five members (no more than three may be from the same political party), who serve seven-year terms. When a term expires, the member may continue to serve until a successor takes office. The President designates the chair. (15 U.S.C. § 41)

FTC Membership as of the End of the 110th Congress.

Incumbent	Party	Date first confirmed	Term expires	Pay level
William E. Kovacic (Chair)	R	12/17/05	09/25/11	III
Pamela J. Harbour	I	07/23/03	09/25/09	IV
Jonathan D. Leibowitz	D	11/21/04	09/25/10	IV
J. Thomas Rosch	R	12/17/05	09/25/12	IV
Vacant			09/25/15	IV

No FTC Appointment Action During the 110th Congress

FOREIGN CLAIMS SETTLEMENT COMMISSION (FCSC)

The FCSC, located in the Department of Justice, consists of three members (political balance is not required), who serve three-year terms. When a term expires, the member may continue to serve until a successor takes office. Only the chair, who also is appointed by the President with the advice and consent of the Senate, serves full-time. (22 U.S.C. §§ 1622, 1622c)

Full-Time FCSC Membership as of the End of the 110th Congress.

Incumbent	Party	Date first confirmed	Term expires	Pay level
Mauricio J. Tamargo (Chair)	na	01/25/02	09/30/09	V

No FCSC Appointment Action to Full-Time Positions During the 110th Congress

Note: A nomination for a part-time position at the Foreign Claims Settlement Commission also occurred during the 110th Congress. This report covers only full-time positions; the part-time nomination is not included in this table.

MERIT SYSTEMS PROTECTION BOARD (MSPB)

The MSPB consists of three members (no more than two may be from the same political party), who serve seven-year terms. A member who has been appointed to a full seven-year term may not be reappointed to any following term. When a term expires, the member may continue to serve for one year, unless a successor is appointed before that time. The President appoints the chair, with the advice and consent of the Senate, and designates the vice chair. (5 U.S.C. §§ 1201-1203)

MSPB Membership as of the End of the 110th Congress.

Incumbent	Party	confirmed	Term expires	level
Neil A. G. McPhie (Chair)	R	11/21/04	03/01/09	III
Mary M. Rose (Vice Chair)	R	12/17/05	03/01/11	IV
Vacant			03/01/14	IV

No MSPB Appointment Action During the 110th Congress

NATIONAL CREDIT UNION ADMINISTRATION BOARD OF DIRECTORS (NCUA)

The NCUA consists of three members (no more than two members may be from the same political party), who serve six-year terms. When a term expires, a member may continue to serve until a successor takes office. The President designates the chair. (12 U.S.C. § 1752a)

NCUA Membership as of the End of the 110th Congress.

Incumbent	Party	Date first confirmed	Term expires	Pay level
Michael E. Fryzel (Chair)	R	06/27/08	08/02/13	III
Rodney E. Hood	R	11/07/05	04/10/09	IV
Gigi Hyland	D	11/07/05	08/02/11	IV

NCUA Appointment Action During the 110th Congress

NATIONAL LABOR RELATIONS BOARD (NLRB)

The NLRB consists of five members, who serve five-year terms. Political balance is not required, but, by tradition, no more than three members are from the same political party. When a term expires, the member must leave office. The President designates the chair. The President also appoints the general counsel, with the advice and consent of the Senate. (29 U.S.C. § 153)

NLRB Membership as of the End of the 110th Congress.

Incumbent	Party	Date first confirmed	Term expires	Pay level
Board				
Peter C. Schaumber (Chair)	R	11/14/02	08/27/10	III
Wilma B. Liebman	D	11/14/02	08/27/11	IV
Vacant			08/27/13	IV
Vacant			12/16/12	IV
Vacant			12/16/09	IV
General Counsel[a]				
Ronald E. Meisburg	na	08/03/06	08/13/10	IV

a. The abbreviation "na" means not applicable. The provision establishing the general counsel position does not include requirements with regard to political affiliation. The general counsel is appointed for a term of four years.

NLRB Appointment Action During the 110th Congress.

Nominee/Recess appointee	Party	Position	To replace	Date nominated	Date confirmed	Days to confirm
Dennis P. Walsh	D	Member	Reappointment	01/09/07	Withdrawn 01/25/08	
Peter N. Kirsanow	R	Member	Ronald E. Meisburg	01/09/07	Withdrawn 01/25/08	
Robert J. Battista	R	Member	Dennis P. Walsh	01/25/08	Withdrawn 05/06/08	
Gerard Morales	R	Member	Robert J. Battista	01/25/08	Returned 01/02/09a	
Dennis P. Walsh	D	Member	Peter N. Kirsanow	01/25/08	Returned 01/02/09a	
Dennis P. Walsh	D	Member	Reappointment	01/25/08	Returned 01/02/09a	

a. Returned to the President at the end of the 110th Congress under the provisions of Senate Rule XXXI, paragraph 6 of the Standing Rules of the Senate.

National Mediation Board (NMB)

The board consists of three members (no more than two may be from the same political party), who serve three-year terms. When a term expires, the member may continue to serve until a successor takes office. The board annually designates a chair. (45 U.S.C. § 154)

NMB Membership as of the End of the 110th Congress.

Incumbent	Party	Date first confirmed	Term expires	Pay level
Read Van de Watera (Chair)	R	12/03/03	07/01/06	III
Elizabeth Dougherty	R	12/09/06	07/01/10	IV
Harry R. Hoglander[a]	D	08/01/02	07/01/08	IV

a. The terms of the incumbents shown in italics had expired. The incumbents continued to serve under the holdover provision noted above.

No NMB Appointment Action During the 110th Congress

National Transportation Safety Board (NTSB)

The NTSB consists of five members (no more than three may be from the same political party), who serve five-year terms. When a term expires, a member may continue to serve until a successor takes office. The President appoints the chair, from among the members, for a two-year term, with the advice and consent of the Senate, and designates the vice chair. (49 U.S.C. § 1111)

NTSB Membership as of the End of the 110th Congress.

Incumbent	Party	Date first confirmed	Term expires	Pay level
Mark V. Rosenker (Acting Chair)	R	03/19/03	12/31/10	III
Robert L. Sumwalt III	R	08/03/06	12/31/11	IV
Deborah A. P. Hersmana	D	03/02/04	12/31/08	IV
Kathryn O. Higgins	D	12/17/05	12/31/09	IV
Steven R. Chealander[a]	R	12/09/06	12/31/07	IV

a. The terms of the incumbents shown in italics had expired. The incumbents continued to serve under the holdover provision noted above.

NTSB Appointment Action During the 110th Congress.

Nominee/Recess appointee	Party	Position	To replace	Date nominated	Date confirmed	Days to confirm
Steven R. Chealander	R	Member	Reappointment	10/26/07	Returned 01/02/09[a]	
Mark V. Rosenker	R	Chair	Reappointment	10/26/07	Returned 01/02/09[a]	
Deborah A. P. Hersman	D	Member	Reappointment	07/31/08	Returned 01/02/09[a]	

a. Returned to the President at the end of the 110th Congress under the provisions of Senate Rule XXXI, paragraph 6 of the Senate.

NUCLEAR REGULATORY COMMISSION (NRC)

The NRC consists of five members (no more than three may be from the same political party), who serve five-year terms. When a term expires, the member must leave office. The President designates the chair. The President also appoints the inspector general, with the advice and consent of the Senate. (42 U.S.C. § 5841 and 5 U.S.C. App., Inspector General Act of 1978, §§ 3, 12)

NRC Membership as of the End of the 110th Congress.

Incumbent	Party	Date first confirmed	Term expires	Pay level
Commissioners				
Dale E. Klein (Chair)	R	05/26/06	06/30/11	II
Gregory B. Jaczko	D	05/26/06	06/30/13	III
Peter B. Lyons	R	05/26/06	06/30/09	III
Kristine L. Svinicki	R	03/13/08	06/30/12	III
Vacant			06/30/10	III
Inspector General				
Hubert T. Bell	na	06/11/96	Indefinite	a

a. The abbreviation "na" means not applicable. The provision establishing the inspector general position does not include requirements with regard to political affiliation. This position does not have a fixed term. As of the end of the 110th Congress, the Inspector General Act provided as follows: "An Inspector General may be removed from office by the President. If an Inspector General is removed from office or is transferred to another position or location within an establishment, the President shall communicate in writing the reasons for any such removal or transfer to both Houses of Congress, not later than 30 days before the removal or transfer. Nothing in [this provision] shall prohibit a personnel action otherwise authorized by law, other than transfer or removal." (5 U.S.C. App., § 3(b)). "The annual rate of basic pay for an Inspector General ... shall be the rate payable for level III of the Executive Schedule ... plus 3 percent." (5 U.S.C. App., § 3 (e)).

NRC Appointment Action During the 110th Congress.

Nominee/ Recess appointee	Party	Position	To replace	Date nominated	Date confirmed	Days to confirm
Kristine L. Svinicki	R	Member	Jeffrey S. Merrifield	04/30/07	03/13/08	318
Gregory B. Jaczko	D	Member	Reappointment	12/04/07	03/13/08	100
Mean number of days to confirm					209	

Occupational Safety and Health Review Commission (OSHRC)

The OSHRC consists of three members (political balance is not required), who serve six-year terms. When a term expires, the member must leave office. The President designates the chair. (29 U.S.C. § 661).

OSHRC Membership as of the End of the 110th Congress.

Incumbent	Party[a]	Date first confirmed	Term expires	Pay level
Horace A. Thompson III (Chair)	na	05/19/06	04/27/11	III
Thomasina Rogers	na	07/31/03	04/27/09	IV
Vacant	na		04/27/13	IV

a The abbreviation "na" means not applicable.

b Returned to the President at the end of the 110th under the provisions of the Senate Rule XXXI, paragraph 6 of the Standing Rules of the Senate.

Postal Regulatory Commission (PRC)

The Postal Rate Commission became the Postal Regulatory Commission, as provided in Section 604 of P.L. 109-435, the Postal Accountability and Enhancement Act, enacted on December 20, 2006.

The commission consists of five members (no more than three may be from the same political party), who serve six-year terms. After a term expires, a member may continue to serve until his successor takes office, but the member may not continue to serve for more than one year after the date upon which his tem otherwise would expire. The President designates the chair, and the members select the vice chair. (39 U.S.C. § 502)

PRC Membership as of the End of the 110th Congress.

Incumbent	Party	Date first confirmed	Term expires	Pay level
Dan G. Blair (Chair)	R	12/09/06	10/14/12	III
Nanci E. Langley (Vice Chair)	D	06/04/08	11/22/12	IV
Mark D. Acton	R	08/03/06	10/14/10	IV
Tony Hammond	R	11/12/02	10/14/10	IV
Ruth Y. Goldway	D	11/12/02	11/22/14	IV

PRC Appointment Action During the 110th Congress.

Nominee/ Recess appointee	Party	Position	To replace	Date nominated	Date confirmed	Days to confirm
Nanci E. Langley	D	Commissioner	Dawn A. Tisdale	02/27/08	06/04/08	98
Ruth Y. Goldway	D	Commissioner	Reappointment	07/10/08	10/02/08	84
Mean number of days to confirm				91		

Privacy and Civil Liberties Oversight Board (PCLOB)

The board consists of five members (no more than three members of the board may be from the same political party), who serve six-year terms. When a term expires, the member may continue to serve until a successor takes office. Only the chair, who also is appointed by the President with the advice and consent of the Senate, serves full-time. (42 § 2000ee)

The Implementing Recommendations of the 9/11 Commission Act of 2007, P.L. 110-53, Title VIII, § 801 (121 Stat. 352) established the Privacy and Civil Liberties Oversight Board, and the first new nominations to the board were made in the 110th Congress. Previously the Privacy and Civil Liberties Oversight Board functioned as part of the White House Office in the Executive Office of the President. That board ceased functioning on January 30, 2008. As of the end of the 110th Congress, the new board had not been constituted. (See CRS Report RL34385, *Privacy and Civil Liberties Oversight Board: New Independent Agency Status*, by Garrett Hatch.)

Full-Time PCLOB Membership as of the End of the 110th Congress.

Incumbent	Party	Date first confirmed	Term expires	Pay level
Vacant (Chair)				III

PCLOB Appointment Action to Full-Time Positions During the 110th Congress.

Nominee/Recess appointee[a]	Party	Position	To replace	Date nominated	Date confirmed	Days to confirm
Daniel W. Sutherland	[b]	Chair	New position	02/27/08	Returned 01/02/09[c]	

a Nominations for a part-time positions at the Privacy and Civil Liberties Oversight Board also occurred during the 110th Congress. This report covers only full-time positions; the part-time nominations are not included in this table.

b Party affiliation is unknown.

c Returned to the President at the end of the 110th Congress under the provisions of Senate Rule XXXI, paragraph 6 of the Standing Rules of the Senate.

RAILROAD RETIREMENT BOARD (RRB)

The board consists of three members (political balance is not required), who serve five-year terms. When a term expires, the member may continue to serve until a successor takes office. The President appoints the chair, and an inspector general, with the advice and consent of the Senate. (45 U.S.C. § 231f and 5 U.S.C. App., Inspector General Act of 1978, §§ 3, 12)

RRB Membership as of the End of the 110th Congress.

Incumbent	Party[a]	Date first confirmed	Term expires	Pay level
Board				
Michael S. Schwartz (Chair; Member-at- Large)	na	05/23/03	08/28/12	III
Virgil M. Speakman Jr. (Labor Member)	na	08/12/92	08/28/09	IV
Jerome F. Kever[b] (Management Member)	na	05/24/00	08/28/08	IV
Inspector General				
Martin J. Dickman	na	10/08/94	Indefinite	c

a The abbreviation "na" means not applicable.

b The term of the incumbent shown in italics had expired. He continued to serve under the holdover provision noted above.

c This position does not have a fixed term. As of the end of the 110th Congress, the Inspector General Act provided as follows: "An Inspector General may be removed from office by the President. If an Inspector General is removed from office or is transferred to another position or location within an establishment, the President shall communicate in writing the reasons for any such removal or transfer to both Houses of Congress, not later than 30 days before the removal or transfer. Nothing in [this provision] shall prohibit a personnel action otherwise authorized by law, other than transfer or removal." (5 U.S.C. App., § 3(b)). "The annual rate of basic pay for an Inspector General ... shall be the rate payable for level III of the Executive Schedule ... plus 3 percent." (5 U.S.C. App., § 3 (e))

RRB Appointment Action During the 110th Congress.

Nominee/Recess appointee	Party[a]	Position	To replace	Date nominated	Date confirmed	Days to confirm
Jerome F. Kever	na	Member	Reappointment	05/22/07	06/22/07	31
Michael S. Schwartz	na	Member	Reappointment	05/22/07	06/22/07	31
Virgil M. Speakman Jr.	na	Member	Reappointment	05/22/07	06/22/07	31

a. The abbreviation "na" means not applicable.

Securities and Exchange Commission (SEC)

The commission consists of five members (no more than three may be from the same political party), who serve five-year terms. When a term expires, the member may continue to serve until the end of the next session of Congress, unless a successor is appointed before that time. The President designates the chair. (15 U.S.C. § 78d)

SEC Membership as of the End of the 110th Congress.

Incumbent	Party	Date first confirmed	Term expires	Pay level
Christopher Cox (Chair)	R	07/29/05	06/05/09	III
Kathleen L. Casey	R	06/15/06	06/05/11	IV
Elisse Walter	D	07/25/02	06/05/12	IV
Luis A. Aguilar	D	07/29/05	06/05/10	IV
Troy A. Paredes	R	06/27/08	06/05/13	IV

SEC Appointment Action During the 110th Congress.

Nominee/ Recess appointee	Party	Position	To replace	Date nominated	Date confirmed	Days to confirm
Elisse Walter	D	Member	Annette L. Nazareth	03/31/08	06/27/08	88
Luis A. Aguilar	D	Member	Roel C. Campos	03/31/08	06/27/08	88
Troy A. Paredes	R	Member	Paul S. Atkins	05/06/08	06/27/08	52
Mean number of days to confirm						76

Surface Transportation Board (STB)

The STB, located within the Department of Transportation, consists of three members (no more than two may be from the same political party), who serve five-year terms. When a term expires, the member may continue to serve until a successor takes office, but not for more than one year after expiration. The President designates the chair. (49 U.S.C. § 701)

STB Membership as of the End of the 110th Congress.

Incumbent	Party	Date first confirmed	Term expires	Pay level
Charles D. Nottingham (Chair)	R	08/03/06	12/31/10	III
Francis P. Mulvey (Vice Chair)	D	05/21/04	12/31/12	IV
W. Douglas Buttreya	R	05/21/04	12/31/08	IV

a. The term of the incumbent shown in italics had expired. He continued to serve under the holdover provision noted above.

STB Appointment Action During the 110th Congress.

Nominee/Recess appointee	Party	Position	To replace	Date nominated	Date confirmed	Days to confirm
Francis P. Mulvey	D	Member	Reappointment	12/03/07	12/19/07	16
Husein A. Cumber	a	Member	W. Douglas Buttrey	05/20/08	Returned 01/02/09b	

a Party affiliation is unknown.

b Returned to the President at the end of the 110th Congress under the provisions of Senate Rule XXXI, paragraph 6 of the Standing Rules of the Senate.

United States International Trade Commission (USITC)

The USITC consists of six members (no more than three may be from the same political party), who serve nine-year terms. A member of the commission who has served for more than five years is ineligible for reappointment. When a term expires, a member may continue to serve until a successor takes office. The President designates the chair and vice chair for two-year terms of office, but they may not belong to the same political party. The President may not designate a chair with less than one year of continuous service as a member. This restriction does not apply to the vice chair. (19 U.S.C. § 1330)

USITC Membership as of the End of the 110th Congress.

Incumbent	Party	Date first confirmed	Term expires	Pay level
Shara L. Aranoff (Chair)	D	07/29/05	12/16/12	III
Daniel R. Pearson (Vice Chair)	R	11/21/04	06/16/11	IV
Deanna T. Okun[a]	R	11/19/99	06/16/08	IV
Charlotte R. Lane	R	11/21/04	12/16/09	IV
Irving A. Williamson	D	02/01/07	06/16/14	IV
Dean A. Pinkert	D	02/01/07	12/16/15	IV

a. The term of the incumbent shown in italics had expired. She continued to serve under the holdover provision noted above.

USITC Appointment Action During the 110th Congress.

Nominee/Recess appointee	Party	Position	To replace	Date nominated	Date confirmed	Days to confirm
Irving A. Williamson	D	Member	Stephen Koplan	01/09/07	02/01/07	23
Dean A. Pinkert	D	Member	Jennifer A. Hillman	01/09/07	02/01/07	23
J. V. Schwan	R	Member	Deanna T. Okun	06/18/08	Returned 01/02/09[a]	

a. Returned to the President at the end of the 110th Congress under the provisions of Senate Rule XXXI, paragraph 6 of the Standing Rules of the Senate.

UNITED STATES PAROLE COMMISSION (USPC)

The USPC is an independent agency in the Department of Justice. The commission consists of five commissioners (political balance is not required), who serve for six-year terms. When a term expires, a member may continue to serve until a successor takes office. In most cases, a commissioner may serve no more than 12 years. However, Section 11017(c) of P.L. 110-273, enacted on November 2, 2002, provides that this limitation does not "apply to a person serving as Commissioner" when the act took effect. The President designates the chair. (18 U.S.C. § 4202)

The commission was previously scheduled to be phased out, but its life has been extended several times by Congress. Under P.L. 110-312, § 2 (122 Stat. 3013), it was extended until November 1, 2011. (18 U.S.C. § 3551)

USPC Membership as of the End of the 110th Congress.

Incumbent	Party[a]	Date first confirmed	Term expires	Pay level
Edward F. Reilly, Jr. (Chair)	na	08/12/91	03/06/09	IV
Cranston J. Mitchell (Vice Chair)	na	03/06/03	03/06/09	V
Patricia Cushwa	na	11/21/04	12/11/10	V
Isaac Fulwood, Jr.	na	11/21/04	12/11/10	V
Vacant	na		na	V

a The abbreviation "na" means not applicable.

USPC Appointment Action During the 110th Congress.

Nominee/ Recess appointee	Party[a]	Position	To replace	Date nominated	Date confirmed	Days to confirm
Dorla M. Salling	na	Member	Deborah A. Spagnoli	01/22/08	Returned 01/02/09[b]	

a The abbreviation "na" mean not applicable.

b Returned to the President at the end of the 110th Congress under the provisions of Senate Rule XXXI paragraph 6 of the Standing Rules of the Senate.

UNITED STATES SENTENCING COMMISSION (USSC)

The USSC is a judicial branch agency that consists of seven voting members, who are appointed to six-year terms, and two non-voting members. The seven voting members are appointed by the President, with the advice and consent of the Senate. Only the chair and three vice chairs, selected from among the members, serve full-time. The President appoints the chair, with the advice and consent of the Senate, and designates the vice chairs. At least three members must be federal judges. Not more than four members may be of the same political party. No more than two vice chairs may be of the same political party. No voting member may serve more than two full terms. When a term expires, an incumbent may continue to serve until he or she is reappointed, a successor takes office, or Congress adjourns *sine die* at the end of the session that commences after the expiration of the term, whichever is earliest. The Attorney General (or designee) serves *ex officio* as a non-voting member. (28 U.S.C. § 991-992) The chair of the United State Parole Commission is also an *ex officio* non-voting member of the commission. (18 U.S.C. § 3551 note)

Full-Time USSC Membership as of the End of the 110th Congress.

Incumbent	Party	Date first confirmed	Term expires	Pay level
Ricardo H. Hinojosa (Chair)	R	11/21/04	10/31/13	Same as rate for federal appeals court judges
Ruben Castillo (Vice Chair)	a	11/10/99	10/31/09	
William K. Sessions III (Vice Chair)	D	11/10/99	10/31/09	
William B. Carr Jr. (Vice Chair)	a	11/20/08	10/31/11	

a. Party balance is statutorily required, as discussed above, but the commission staff does not collect this information. For this member, alternative sources of information could not be located.

USSC Appointment Action to Full-Time Positions During the 110th Congress.

Nominee/Recess appointee	Party	Position	To replace	Date nominated	Date confirmed	Days to confirm
John R. Steer	R	Member	Reappointment	01/09/07	Withdrawn 06/04/08	
Ricardo H. Hinojosa	R	Chair	Reappointment	12/06/07	Returned 01/02/09	
Ricardo H. Hinojosa	R	Member	Reappointment	12/06/07	11/20/08	350
William B. Carr Jr.	a	Member	John R. Steer	06/04/08	11/20/08	169
Mean number of days to confirm					260	

a. Party affiliation is unknown.

Appendix A. Summary of All Nominations and Appointments to Collegial Boards and Commissions

Table A-1. Nominations and Appointments to Full-Time Positions on Regulatory and Other Boards and Commissions, 110th Congress.

Nominee/recess appointee	Board/ Commission[a]	Nomination date	Final disposition date	Days to confirm
Jonathan S. Adelstein	FCC	12/03/07	Returned 01/02/09	
Luis A. Aguilar	SEC	03/31/08	06/27/08	88
A. Paul Anderson	FMC	08/02/07	Withdrawn 05/20/08	
Joseph F. Bader	DNFSB	06/26/08	Returned 01/02/09	
Constance S. Barker	EEOC	03/31/08	06/27/08	88
Michael E. Baroody	CPSC	03/05/07	Withdrawn 05/23/07	
(Commissioner)				
Michael E. Baroody (Chair)	CPSC	03/05/07	Withdrawn 05/23/07	
Robert J. Battista	NLRB	01/25/08	Withdrawn 05/06/08	
Cynthia L. Bauerly	FEC	05/06/08	06/24/08	49
Gineen B. Beach	EAC	07/31/08	10/02/08	63
Thomas M. Beck	FLRA	06/28/07	Withdrawn 12/14/07	
Thomas M. Beck	FLRA	12/14/07	10/02/08	293
Wayne C. Beyer	FLRA	01/09/07	Withdrawn 12/14/07	
John S. Bresland (Member)	CSB	07/11/07	03/13/08	246
John S. Bresland (Chair)	CSB	07/11/07	03/13/08	246
Brandon C. Bungard	FLRA	04/02/08	Returned 01/02/09	
Dale Cabaniss	FLRA	03/12/07	Withdrawn 06/28/07	
William B. Carr Jr.	USSC	06/04/08	11/20/08	169
Steven R. Chealander	NTSB	10/26/07	Returned 01/02/09	
Bartholomew H. Chilton	CFTC	05/03/07	08/01/07	90
Bartholomew H. Chilton	CFTC	04/03/08	Returned 01/02/09	

Table A-1. (Continued).

Nominee/recess appointee	Board/ Commission[a]	Nomination date	Final disposition date	Days to confirm
Robert F. Cohen Jr.	FMSHRC	12/12/07	03/13/08	92
Sean T. Connaughton	FMC	09/09/08	Returned 01/02/09	
Husein A. Cumber	STB	05/20/08	Returned 01/02/09	
Donetta Davidson	EAC	05/08/08	10/02/08	147
M. Cynthia Douglass	OSHRC	09/27/07	Returned 01/02/09	
Michael F. Duffy	FMSHRC	01/09/07	03/13/08	429
Elizabeth A. Duke	FRS	05/16/07	06/27/08	408
Diane G. Farrell	EXIMBANK	05/24/07	08/01/07	69
Michael E. Fryzel	NCUA	12/03/07	06/27/08	207
Ruth Y. Goldway	PRC	07/10/08	10/02/08 84	
Deborah A. P. Hersman	NTSB	07/31/08	Returned 01/02/09	
Gracia M. Hillman	EAC	06/13/07	10/02/08	477
Ricardo H. Hinojosa (Member)	USSC	12/06/07	11/20/08	350
Ricardo H. Hinojosa (Chair)	USSC	12/06/07	Returned 01/02/09	
Arlene Holen	FMSHRC	01/09/07	Withdrawn 05/20/08	
Caroline C. Hunter	EAC	01/09/07	02/15/07	37
Caroline C. Hunter	FEC	05/06/08	06/24/08	49
Stuart Ishimaru	EEOC	08/03/07	12/19/07	138
Gregory B. Jaczko	NRC	12/04/07	03/13/08	100
Mary L. Jordan	FMSHRC	06/26/08	10/02/08	98
Mark E. Keenum	FCA	06/26/08	Returned 01/02/09	
Joseph T. Kelliher	FERC	03/07/07	12/19/07	287
Jerome F. Kever	RRB	05/22/07	06/22/07	31
Peter N. Kirsanow	NLRB	01/09/07	Withdrawn 01/25/08	
Larry A. Klane	FRS	05/16/07	Returned 01/02/09	
Carl B. Kress	FMC	08/02/07	Returned 01/02/09	
Randall S. Kroszner	FRS	05/16/07	Returned 01/02/09	

Nominee/recess appointee	Board/ Commission[a]	Nomination date	Final disposition date	Days to confirm
Nanci E. Langley	PRC	02/27/08	06/04/08	98
Robert D. Lenhard	FEC	01/09/07	Withdrawn 05/06/08	
Walter Lukken	CFTC	08/07/07	Returned 01/02/09	
David M. Mason	FEC	01/09/07	Withdrawn 05/06/08	
Donald F. McGahn II	FEC	05/06/08	06/24/08	49
Allan I. Mendelowitz	FHFB	10/18/07	12/19/07	62
Gerard Morales	NLRB	01/25/08	Returned 01/02/09	
Francis P. Mulvey	STB	12/03/07	12/19/07	16
Scott O'Malia	CFTC	04/03/08	Returned 01/02/09	
David Palmer	EEOC	01/09/07	Withdrawn 09/04/07	
Troy A. Paredes	SEC	05/06/08	06/27/08	52
Matthew S. Petersen	FEC	06/12/08	06/24/08	12
Dean A. Pinkert	USITC	01/09/07	02/01/07	23
Carol W. Pope	FLRA	03/12/07	Returned 01/02/09	
Carol W. Pope	FLRA	Recess Appointment 04/04/07		
Carol W. Pope	FLRA	05/16/07	10/02/08	505
Bijan Rafiekian	EXIMBANK	02/16/07	08/01/07	166
Rosemary E. Rodriguez	EAC	01/09/07	02/15/07	37
Rosemary E. Rodriguez	EAC	05/08/08	10/02/08	147
Mark V. Rosenker	NTSB	10/26/07	Returned 01/02/09	
Dorla M. Salling	USPC	01/22/08	Returned 01/02/09	
Ambrose L. Schwallie	DNFSB	07/23/08	Returned 01/02/09	
J. V. Schwan	USITC	06/18/08	Returned 01/02/09	
Michael S. Schwartz	RRB	05/22/07	06/22/07	31
Charles R. H. Shearer	CSB	07/11/07	Returned 01/02/09	
Jill E. Sommers	CFTC	05/03/07	08/01/07	90
Nominee/recess appointee	Board/ Commission[a]	Nomination date	Final disposition date	Days to confirm

Table A-1. (Continued).

Hans von Spakovsky	FEC	01/09/07	Withdrawn 05/20/08	
Virgil M. Speakman Jr.	RRB	05/22/07	06/22/07	31
John R. Steer	USSC	01/09/07	Withdrawn 06/04/08	
David W. Sutherland	PCLOB	02/27/08	Returned 01/02/09	
Kristine L. Svinicki	NRC	04/30/07	03/13/08	318
Michael W. Tankersley	EXIMBANK	01/09/07	06/28/07	170
Deborah T. Tate	FCC	06/21/07	Returned 01/02/09	
Dennis P. Walsh	NLRB	01/09/07	Withdrawn 01/25/08	
Dennis P. Walsh	NLRB	01/25/08	Returned 01/02/09	
Dennis P. Walsh	NLRB	01/25/08	Returned 01/02/09	
Elisse Walter	SEC	03/31/08	06/27/08	88
Steven T. Walther	FEC	01/09/07	06/24/08	532
Jon Wellinghoff	FERC	12/11/07	12/19/07	8
Irving A. Williamson	USITC	01/09/07	02/01/07	23
Michael G. Young	FMSHRC	09/08/08	10/02/08	24
Mean number of days to confirm				148
Median number of days to confirm				90

a. The key to the agency acronyms may be found in Appendix C.

Table A-2. Appointment Action, Regulatory and Other Collegial Boards and Commissions, 110th Congress.

Agency[a]	Total Positions	Vacant positions[b]	Incumbent serving; term expired	Nominations submitted	Individual nominees	Positions to which nominations were made[c]	Nominations confirmed	Nominations returned	Nominations withdrawn	Recess appointments
CSB	5	1	0	3	2	3	2	1	0	0
CFTC	5	1	1	5	4	4	2	3	0	0
CPSC	5	3	0	2	1	2	0	0	2	0
DNFSB	5	0	0	2	2	2	0	2	0	0
EAC	4	0	0	6	5	4	6	0	0	0
EEOC	6	1	0	3	3	2	2	0	1	0
EXIMBANK	6	0	0	3	3	3	3	0	0	0
FCA	3	0	1	1	1	1	0	1	0	0
FCC	5	0	2	2	2	2	0	2	0	0
FDIC	4	0	0	0	0	0	0	0	0	0
FEC	6	0	1	8	8	5	5	0	3	0
FERC	5	0	0	2	2	2	2	0	0	0
FHFB	4	0	0	1	1	1	1	0	0	0
FLRA	4	2	0	7	5	4	2	2	3	1
FMC	5	2	1	3	3	2	0	2	1	0
FMSHRC	5	1	0	5	5	5	4	0	1	0
FRS	7	2	1	3	3	3	1	2	0	0
FTC	5	1	0	0	0	0	0	0	0	0

Table A-2. (Continued).

Agency[a]	Total Positions	Vacant positions[b]	Incumbent serving; term expired	Nominations submitted	Individual nominees	Positions to which nominations were made[c]	Nominations confirmed	Nominations returned	Nominations withdrawn	Recess appointments
FCSC	1	0	0	0	0	0	0	0	0	0
MSPB	3	1	0	0	0	0	0	0	0	0
NCUA	3	0	1	1	1	1	1	0	0	0
NLRB	6	3	0	6	4	3	0	3	3	0
NMB	3	0	2	0	0	0	0	0	0	0
NTSB	5	0	2	3	3	3	0	3	0	0
NRC	6	1	0	2	2	2	2	0	0	0
OSHRC	3	1	0	1	1	1	0	1	0	0
PRC	5	0	0	2	2	2	2	0	0	0
PCLOB	1	1	0	1	1	1	0	1	0	0
RRB	4	0	1	3	3	3	3	0	0	0
SEC	5	0	0	3	3	3	3	0	0	0
STB	3	0	1	2	2	2	1	1	0	0
USITC	6	0	1	3	3	3	2	1	0	0
USPC	5	1	0	1	1	1	0	1	0	0

Agency[a]	Total Positions	Vacant positions[b]	Incumbent serving; term expired	Nominations submitted	Individual nominees	Positions to which nominations were made[c]	Nominations confirmed	Nominations returned	Nominations withdrawn	Recess appointments
USSC	4	0	0	4	3	4	2	1	1	0
Total	**152**	**22**	**15**	**88**	**79**	**74**	**46**	**27**	**15**	**1**

a A list of abbreviations may be found in **Appendix C**.

b As of the end of the 110th Congress.

c For some agencies, appointment of an individual to be chair requires two separate nominations: one to be a member and the other to be chair. This column counts such instances as **two** positions to which nominations were made. For those agencies in which members have fixed terms, a single individual may be nominated for successive terms in a single membership seat. This column counts such instances as **one** position to which a nomination was made.

Appendix B. Senate Recesses and Presidential Recess Appointments

Table B-1. Senate Intersession Recesses, Intrasession Recesses of Four or More Days, and Numbers of Recess Appointments to Positions on Regulatory and Other Collegial Boards and Commissions, 110th Congress.

Date recessed	Date reconvened	Number of days adjourneda	Number of recess appointments to specified positions
(The first session of the 110th Congress convened on January 4, 2007.)			
02/17/07	02/26/07	9	0
03/29/07	04/10/07	12	1
05/25/07	06/04/07	10	0
06/29/07	07/09/07	10	0
08/03/07	09/04/07	32	0
10/05/07	10/15/07	10	0

The Senate adjourned sine die on December 31, 2007. The second session of the 110th Congress convened on January 3, 2008. The intersession (period between these two dates) was three days long.[a] There were no intrasession recesses of four or more days during the 110th Congress, 2nd session. The Senate adjourned its second session on January 2, 2009.

Source: Table created by the Congressional Research Service using data from the *Congressional Record.*

Note: For the purposes of determining the length of an intrasession recess for inclusion in this table, Sundays were not counted. Under congressional precedents, Sunday is considered a "dies non," or a day on which Congress is not expected to meet, for purposes of determining whether Congress has adjourned for "not more than three days."

a. The number of days adjourned was counted starting on the first calendar day after an adjournment and ending on the day of reconvening, including in the count the day the Senate reconvened. This is consistent with the House practice for counting recess days for the purposes of meeting congressional adjournment requirements in the Constitution ("Neither House, during the Session of Congress, shall, without the Consent of the other, adjourn for more than three days ...." Art. I, § 5, cl. 4). Under House precedents, "The House of Representatives in adjourning for not more than three days must take into the count either the day of adjourning or the day of the meeting, and Sunday is not taken into account in making this computation" U.S. Congress, House, *Constitution, Jefferson's Manual and Rules of the House of Representatives of the United States, One Hundred Tenth Congress*, 109th Cong., 2nd sess., H.Doc. 109-157 (Washington: GPO, 2007), p. 37. Senate practice appears to be consistent with this approach (Floyd M. Riddick and

Alan S. Frumin, *Riddick's Senate Procedure: Precedents and Practices*, 101st Cong., 2nd sess., S.Doc. 101-28, (Washington: GPO, 1992), pp. 15-16). Inasmuch as it has been argued that the periods during which the President could make recess appointments might be those in which the Senate is in recess pursuant to the constitutional provision just quoted, it appears that this method of calculating recess days would provide a relevant measure of recess length in the context of discussions of recess appointments. Other methods might be used in other contexts. For example, a method in which neither the day of adjournment nor the day of reconvening were counted has been used elsewhere. This method takes into account that the Senate could act on nominations on either of these days, obviating the need for a recess appointment.

APPENDIX C. BOARD/COMMISSION ABBREVIATIONS

CSB	Chemical Safety and Hazard Investigation Board
CFTC	Commodity Futures Trading Commission
CPSC	Consumer Product Safety Commission
DNFSB	Defense Nuclear Facilities Safety Board
EAC	Election Assistance Commission
EEOC	Equal Employment Opportunity Commission
EXIMBANK	Export-Import Bank
FCA	Farm Credit Administration
FCC	Federal Communications Commission
FDIC	Federal Deposit Insurance Corporation, Board of Directors
FEC	Federal Election Commission
FERC	Federal Energy Regulatory Commission
FHFB	Federal Housing Finance Board
FLRA	Federal Labor Relations Authority
FMC	Federal Maritime Commission
FMSHRC	Federal Mine Safety and Health Review Commission
FRS	Federal Reserve System, Board of Governors
FTC	Federal Trade Commission
FCSC	Foreign Claims Settlement Commission
MSPB	Merit Systems Protection Board
NCUA	National Credit Union Administration, Board of Directors
NLRB	National Labor Relations Board
NMB	National Mediation Board
NTSB	National Transportation Safety Board
NRC	Nuclear Regulatory Commission

OSHRC	Occupational Safety and Health Review Commission
PRC	Postal Regulatory Commission
PCLOB	Privacy and Civil Liberties Oversight Board
RRB	Railroad Retirement Board
SEC	Securities and Exchange Commission
STB	Surface Transportation Board
USITC	United States International Trade Commission
USPC	United States Parole Commission
USSC	United States Sentencing Commission

APPENDIX D. CHANGE IN METHODOLOGY FROM PREVIOUS TRACKING REPORTS

The calculations of nomination-to-confirmation intervals provided in this report counted all the days within the interval, including those during summer recesses and between sessions of the Senate. The inclusion of all days differs from the methodology used in similar CRS reports for previous Congresses.[31] In these earlier reports, days during August and intersession recesses were not included in calculations of nomination-to-confirmation intervals. The rationale for the earlier methodology was that the Senate was unlikely to continue consideration of nominations during these periods; committee hearings and votes, among other activities, typically do not occur during these times. The exclusion of days during only certain periods of adjournment—intersession recesses and August recesses, which are usually longer than 30 days—is suggested by Senate rules regarding when nominations are to be returned to the President. These provide:

> Nominations neither confirmed nor rejected during the session at which they are made shall not be acted upon at any succeeding session without being again made to the Senate by the President; and if the Senate shall adjourn or take recess for more than thirty days, all nominations pending and not finally acted upon at the time of taking such adjournment or recess shall be returned by the Secretary to the President.[32]

This earlier methodology was also consistent with the approach of some political scientists who study executive branch appointments.[33]

The methodology for this report is different from that which was used in previous similar reports for several reasons. First, as discussed above in the section on recess appointments, from the latter part of the first session through the end of the 110th Congress, the Senate chose to break up what would otherwise have been longer recesses into shorter recesses separated by pro forma sessions. This introduced two options for this report with regard to the calculation of nomination-toconfirmation intervals. The first option would have been to treat each series of short recesses created in this fashion as one long recess and to subtract these days from the nomination-toconfirmation interval.[34] The second option would have been to treat each recess in the series of short recesses created in this fashion as a short recess, and not to subtract these days from the nomination-to-confirmation interval. Arguably, the Senate and President actions were consistent with the latter construction—short recesses as short recesses. Otherwise, Senate rules would have required the return of pending nominations (or the waiver of that rule),[35] and the President could have—and likely would have—made recess appointments. The Senate and the President did not take these actions. Because of this, short recesses created by pro forma sessions are treated as short recesses in this report. It should be noted, however, that this reduces the comparability of statistics provided in this report with statistics in previous similar tracking reports, since the intervals calculated in this report include days that, in previous reports, were part of longer recesses and therefore were subtracted from the length of the interval. Although the phenomenon underlying this methodological problem first arose during the 110th Congress, it could arise again in future Congresses.

Other reasons for the methodological change are not unique to the 110th Congress. First, in some cases, committee or floor action on a nomination that could have been completed before a recess has been, instead, deferred until after the recess. For such a nomination, the period of Senate consideration arguably has been intentionally extended. Counting all days, including those during a long recess, in calculations of elapsed time reflects that extension of Senate consideration. Second, it is unlikely that all work pertaining to nominations stops over a recess, and the inclusion of recess days is a reflection of the fact that the nominee is still under consideration, even during recess. Member and committee staffs may still be considering nominations at that time, even though they may not take direct action in the form of hearings or votes on the nominees. Ongoing activities may include investigatory work and interviews with nominees. Finally, although, as mentioned above, some political scientists who study nominations do subtract recess days during calculations of nomination-to-confirmation intervals, many others do not.[36] In addition, the calculation of nomination-to-confirmation intervals in CRS research concerning judicial nominations does not exclude days that fall during recesses. By using methodology that is more similar to the work of other political scientists and to CRS judicial nominations research, the research presented here could be more easily compared and combined with related work. For all of these reasons, in this report, we employ a new methodology for calculating nomination-to-confirmation intervals.

End Notes

[1] A succinct historical and contemporary overview of the appointment power is found in Louis Fisher, "Appointment Powers," in his *Constitutional Conflicts between Congress and the President*, 5th ed. (Lawrence, KS: University Press of Kansas, 2007), pp. 21-47.

[2] Article II, § 2, cl. 2, provides that the President "shall nominate, and by and with the Advice and Consent of the Senate, shall appoint Ambassadors, other public Ministers and Consuls, Judges of the supreme Court, and all other Officers of the United States, whose Appointments are not herein otherwise provided for, and which shall be established by Law: but the Congress may by Law vest the Appointment of such inferior Officers, as they think proper, in the President alone, in the Courts of Law, or in the Heads of Departments."

[3] Since the ratification of the Twentieth Amendment to the Constitution, on January 23, 1933, the terms of the President and Vice President expire at noon on January 20 following a presidential election. Prior to this change, presidential transitions occurred on March 4 following a presidential election. Arguably, the growth in the number of presidentially appointed positions and the shorter period between election and inauguration of a new President has intensified the transition period appointment bottleneck and its impact. On the other hand, aspects of this process have probably been eased by improvements in transportation that have allowed elected officials and appointees to more quickly travel to the capital after an election, and by improvements in communication and information technology that have facilitated more rapid exchanges of appointment-related information.

[4] 3 U.S.C. 102 note.

[5] For more on the role of Senators in the appointment of U.S. district judges, see CRS Report RL34405, *Role of Home State Senators in the Selection of Lower Federal Court Judges*, by Denis Steven Rutkus.

[15] For a further information, see CRS Report RS21308, *Recess Appointments: Frequently Asked Questions*, by Henry B. Hogue.

[16] P.L. 110-161, Div. D, § 709; 121 Stat. 2021. The provision reads: "Hereafter, no part of any appropriation contained in this or any other Act shall be paid to any person for the filling of any position for which he or she has been nominated after the Senate has voted not to approve the nomination of said person." This provision has been part of this funding bill since at least 1950.

[17] *Mackie v. Clinton*, Memorandum of Points and Authorities in Support of Defendants' Opposition to Plaintiffs' Motion for Partial Summary Judgment, at 24-26, Civ. Action No. 93-0032-LFO, (D.D.C. 1993).

[18] Although, as described here, the Senate majority leader initially indicated that the use of pro forma sessions was intended to prevent the President from making recess appointments, on at least one other occasion, he provided another reason for using these sessions. On September 17, 2008, he announced, with regard to the Senate, "We are going to have to get some committee hearings underway, which is why we are not going to adjourn. We will be in pro forma session so committees can still meet, though we won't have any activities here on the floor as relates to these markets."

(Sen. Harry Reid, "The Economy," remarks in the Senate, *Congressional Record*, daily edition, vol. 154 (September
17, 2008), p. S8907.)

[19] Sen. Harry Reid, "Recess Appointments," remarks in the Senate, *Congressional Record*, daily edition, vol. 153
(November 16, 2007), p. S14609.

[20] A pro forma session is a short meeting of the House or Senate during which it is understood that no business will be conducted.

[21] For specific instances, see CRS Report RL33310, *Recess Appointments Made by President George W. Bush*, by Henry B. Hogue and Maureen Bearden.

[22] Exceptions are as follows: (1) the Federal Energy Regulatory Commission (FERC), located in the Department of Energy (DOE); (2) the Foreign Claims Settlement Commission (FCSC) and (3) the United States Parole Commission (USPC), both located in the Department of Justice (DOJ); and (4) the Surface Transportation Board (STB), located in the

Department of Transportation (DOT). FERC's enabling statute designated it as an independent entity in DOE, and provided that its members and employees are not subject to the supervision or direction of department officials (42 U.S.C. § 7171(d)). The FCSC was designated as an independent entity within DOJ, with a specific provision that decisions of the commission with respect to claims shall not be subject to review by the Attorney General (22 U.S.C. § 1622g). The enabling statute of the STB provided that "members, employees, and other personnel of the Board shall not be responsible to or subject to the supervision or direction of any officer, employee, or agent" of DOT (49 U.S.C. § 703(c)). The enabling statute of the USPC established it is an independent agency within the Department of Justice (18 U.S.C. § 4202).

[23] In contrast, for a few agencies, such as the Chemical Safety and Hazard Investigation Board, the full term begins to run when an appointee takes office, and it expires after the incumbent has held the post for the requisite period of time.

[24] For 3 of these 26 organizations, the Election Assistance Commission, the Federal Election Commission, and the United States International Trade Commission, the number of member positions is even, and no more than half may be of the same party.

[25] The enabling statutes for some boards and commissions provide for the continuation of a member's service past the end of his or her term for an additional specified period of time, or until replaced by a successor. Such provisions are known as holdover provisions. A member of the Defense Nuclear Facilities Safety Board, for example, serves for a term of five years, but "may serve after the expiration of that member's term until a successor has taken office" (42 U.S.C. § 2286(d)(3)).

[26] This median is the middle number when the "days to confirm" data for all the confirmed nominations are arranged in numerical order.

[27] See, for example, CRS Report RL34744, *Presidential Appointments to Full-Time Positions on Regulatory and Other Collegial Boards and Commissions, 109th Congress*, by Henry B. Hogue et al.

[28] This report was compiled from data from the Senate nominations database of the Legislative Information System http://www.congress.gov/nomis/, telephone discussions with agency officials, agency websites, the United States Code, and the 2008 "Plum Book" (U.S. Congress, Senate Committee on Homeland Security and Governmental Affairs, *United States Government Policy and Supporting Positions*, 110th Cong., 2nd sess., Committee Print, November 12, 2008 (Washington: GPO, 2008)).

[29] The pay rates for the Executive Schedule, as of the end of the 110th Congress (2008), were as follows: Level I, $191,300; Level II, $172,200; Level III, $158,500; Level IV, $149,000; and Level V, $139,600. U.S. Office of Personnel Management "Salary Table 2008-EX," available at http://www.opm.gov/oca/08tables/html/ex.asp.

[30] This median is the middle number when the "days to confirm" data for all the confirmed nominations are arranged in numerical order.

[6] P.L. 105-277, Div. C, Title I, sec. 151; 5 U.S.C. § 3345-3349d. For more on the Federal Vacancies Reform Act of 1998, see CRS Report 98-892, *The New Vacancies Act: Congress Acts to Protect the Senate's Confirmation Prerogative*, by Morton Rosenberg.

[7] 5 U.S.C. § 3349c.

[8] For further information, see CRS Report RL31980, *Senate Consideration of Presidential Nominations: Committee and Floor Procedure*, by Elizabeth Rybicki, and CRS Report RL31948, *Evolution of the Senate's Role in the Nomination and Confirmation Process: A Brief History*, by Betsy Palmer.

[9] G. Calvin Mackenzie, *The Politics of Presidential Appointments* (New York: The Free Press, 1981), pp. 97-189.

[10] For more, see CRS Report RL30959, *Presidential Appointee Positions Requiring Senate Confirmation and Committees Handling Nominations*, by Henry B. Hogue, Maureen Bearden, and Terrence L. Lisbeth.

[11] For more information, see CRS Report RL31980, *Senate Consideration of Presidential Nominations: Committee and Floor Procedure*, by Elizabeth Rybicki.

[12] The rule may be found in U.S. Congress, Senate Committee on Rules and Administration, *Senate Manual*, 110th Cong., 2nd sess., S. Doc. 110-1 (Washington: GPO, 2008), p. 58, Rule XXXI, paragraph 6 of the Standing Rules of the Senate. For an example of a waiver of the rule, see Sen. William H. Frist, "Nomination to Remain in Status Quo," Congressional Record, daily edition, vol. 152, September 29, 2006, p. S10762.

[13] Art. II, § 2, cl. 3.

[14] Information on other recess appointments during the Administration of President George W. Bush may be found in CRS Report RL33310, *Recess Appointments Made by President George W. Bush*, by Henry B. Hogue and Maureen Bearden.

[31] See, for example, CRS Report RL34744, *Presidential Appointments to Full-Time Positions on Regulatory and Other Collegial Boards and Commissions, 109th Congress*, by Henry B. Hogue et al.

[32] U.S. Congress, Senate Committee on Rules and Administration, *Senate Manual*, 110th Cong., 2nd sess., S.Doc. 110-1 (Washington: GPO, 2008), p. 58, Rule XXXI, paragraph 6 of the Standing Rules of the Senate.

[33] For example, see Nolan McCarty and Rose Razaghian, "Advice and Consent: Senate Responses to Executive Branch Nominations 1885-1996," *American Journal of Political Science*, vol. 43, no. 4 (October 1999), pp. 1122-1143.

[34] This appears to be the construction adopted by the *Congressional Directory*. See U.S. Congress, Joint Committee on Printing, *Congressional Directory, 2009-2010,* 111th Cong., 1st sess., S. Pub. 111-14 (Washington: GPO, 2009), p. 541.

[35] As noted above, under Senate rules, if a nomination is not acted upon by the Senate by the end of a Congress, it is returned to the President. Pending nominations also may be returned automatically to the President at the beginning of a recess of more than 30 days, but the Senate rule providing for this return is often waived. The applicable Senate rule may be found in U.S. Congress, Senate Committee on Rules and Administration, *Senate Manual*, 110th Cong., 2nd sess., S. Doc. 110-1 (Washington: GPO, 2008), p. 58, Rule XXXI, paragraph 6 of the Standing Rules of the Senate.

[36] For example, see Lauren Cohen Bell, "Senatorial Discourtesy: The Senate's Use of Delay to Shape the Federal Judiciary," *Political Research Quarterly*, vol. 55, no. 3 (September 2002), pp. 589-607; Sarah A. Binder and Forrest Maltzman, "Senatorial Delay in Confirming Federal Judges, 1947-1998," *American Journal of Political Science*, vol. 46, no. 1 (January 2002), pp. 190-199; and Karl DeRouen Jr., Jeffrey S. Peake, and Kenneth Ward, "Presidential Mandates and the Dynamics of Senate Advice and Consent, 1885-1996," *American Politics Research*, vol. 33, no. 1 (January 2005), pp. 106-131.

CHAPTER SOURCES

Chapter 1 - This is an edited, reformatted and augmented version of a Congressional Research Service publication, R41497, dated November 19, 2010.

Chapter 2 - This is an edited, reformatted and augmented version of a Congressional Research Service publication, R41463, dated October 25, 2010.

INDEX